30119 012270122

London Borough of Sutton

KV-638-136

As

WA

HANDBOOK OF SPORTS AND RECREATIONAL BUILDING DESIGN

Volume 4 Sports data

THE SPORTS COUNCIL
TECHNICAL UNIT FOR SPORT

Edited by Geraint John and Helen Heard

THE ARCHITECTURAL PRESS · LONDON

AHW R70602   **VOLUME 4**

First published in book form by The Architectural Press Ltd: London 1981
© The Sports Council 1981

Reprinted 1986, 1987

British Library Cataloguing in Publication Data
Sports Council
   Handbook of sports and recreational building design.
  Vol. 4
  1. Recreation centres 2. Sports facilities
  I. Title II. John, Geraint III. Heard, Helen
  725′.8   NA6800

ISBN 0–85139–599–6 (this volume)
ISBN 0–85139–600–3 (complete set)

All rights reserved. No part of this publication may be reproduced, stored in a
retrieval system, or transmitted, in any form or by any means, electronic, mechanical, photocopying, recording or otherwise, without prior permission of the
publishers. Such permission, if granted, is subject to a fee, depending on the nature
of the use.

WA

LONDON BOROUGH
OF SUTTON
PUBLIC LIBRARIES

0122701 22
MAY 1989

R725.8

Printed and bound in Great Britain
at the University Press, Cambridge

Series contents

Volume 1 Ice rinks and swimming pools

Volume 2 Indoor sports

Volume 3 Outdoor sports

Volume 4 Sports data

A note about the Sports Council

The Sports Council is an independent body, established by Royal Charter in 1972 to replace the previous advisory Sports Council, formed in 1965. There are separate Councils for Scotland, Wales and Northern Ireland, though all four work closely to ensure a consistent approach to common problems. The Sports Council has overall responsibility for British sports matters, as well as domestic affairs for England. There are 9 Regional Councils for Sport and Recreation in England. The aims of the Sports Council are to:

● Promote general understanding of the social importance and value of sport and physical recreation
● Increase provision of new sports facilities and stimulate fuller use of existing facilities
● Encourage wider participation in sport and physical recreation as a means of enjoying leisure
● Raise standards of performance.

The Sports Council's Technical Unit for Sport (TUS), which has written the major part of this book, is a group of architects, quantity surveyors and a building services engineer who advise on sport and recreational buildings.

The Technical Unit for Sport of the Sports Council. Key:
1 Geraint John 2 Michael Earle 3 Jennifer Millest
4 David Butler 5 John Davies 6 Chris Harper
7 Margaret Falconer 8 David Edmonds 9 Robin Wilson
10 Anona Robertson 11 Clare Dixon 12 Peter Ackroyd

Photo: Michael Bradley

Foreword

This handbook is the result of more than four years of hard work by our Technical Unit for Sport working closely with the staff of *The Architects' Journal*. It is the largest and most ambitious undertaking of its kind, and I would like to thank The Architectural Press for its enthusiasm and consistent back-up for the project.

In 1972, when the Sports Council published *Provision for Sport*, stressing the urgent need for more and better designed facilities for sport and recreation, it was regarded by some people as a Utopian pipe-dream. Although tremendous progress has been made since then, this must not lead to complacency for in many areas of the country facilities are still inadequate—or even non-existent.

How we face up to this challenge will affect the quality of life and the health of people in Britain for generations to come. Shorter working hours, more mobility and, for most people, more money, have combined to produce the record demand for leisure facilities we have today. Increased leisure time and wider horizons have to be catered for with the right facilities. Time off can be time wasted if the facilities are not there for people to use and enjoy.

This is why I unreservedly welcome the publication of this handbook covering, as it does, a wide range of sports and recreation buildings with the emphasis on provision for the general community.

A new textbook on recreational building design, written by acknowledged experts is long overdue. Properly designed buildings, offering a wide range of use, capable of withstanding prolonged wear and tear and economic to construct and operate, are essential if we are to meet the nation's leisure demands.

Dick Jeeps CBE
Chairman, Sports Council

Acknowledgements

We would like to thank the following for their help: Sports Council for Wales, the Scottish Sports Council and the Sports Council for Northern Ireland; the UK governing bodies of sport, with contributions from many officials and national coaches; John Holborn and Jean Wenger of the National Playing Fields Association; the Sports Council's Sports Development and Facilities Units and the Sports Council Information Centre; the sports equipment trade; local authority officers, recreational consultants, architects and many others who have supplied illustrations.

Data Sheets 27 and 28 (athletics) were based on material prepared by Phil Johnson of the AAA Indoor Development Committee and Hywell Griffiths of the Sports Council. We also gratefully acknowledge earlier development work in this relatively new field of indoor provision carried out in unbuilt projects by the Birmingham City Architects' Department, the Greater London Council, Edinburgh City Council and the other local authorities mentioned in the Data Sheets. For comments and advice on Data Sheet 28 we would like to thank Arthur Gold, CBE, President of the European Athletics Association.

Finally we would like to thank the National Playing Fields Association; diagrams setting out field layouts for the following outdoor sports are based on information which they very kindly made available: athletics, lawn bowls, cricket, crown green bowling, association football, hockey and mini-hockey, lacrosse (men and women's), lawn tennis, netball, Rugby League football, and Rugby Union football.

Introduction

In this volume, Peter Ackroyd has compiled an A–Z of sports Data Sheets in collaboration with the governing bodies of sports and many others who are gratefully acknowledged on p *viii*.

1 Scope

The following Data Sheets give fundamental technical information for the 111 sports and different disciplines covered in the three groups which make up this volume. The games and sports are divided into:

Part I: Indoor activities which can be played in common spaces

Part II: Indoor activities which essentially require a separate or exclusive space

Part III: Outdoor activities

It should be noted, however, that a number of the activities in Part II can take place in common spaces, subject to especially critical considerations such as the size and proportions of the hall, wear and tear of the floor and wall surfaces, additional safety precautions, fitments, storage spaces and other particular requirements. These activities are: athletics indoor competitive, athletics training, darts, gymnastics training pits, roller sports and weight training.

Basic dimensions of the space required for each game and sport are tabulated under the three standards of play commonly referred to:

N: international and national

C: county and club

R: recreational

Where appropriate additional columns are included for Olympic dimensions. The minimum spaces required for each standard of play now fully take into account any necessary run-out or safety margins, team bench and officials' control spaces around the playing area. These together amount to the overall areas given in the tables, and are shown by a broken line surrounding the space diagram on each Data Sheet.

Readers should also refer to Volume 2, Part I, Technical Study **4** for dimensions of sports halls. Volume 2, Part II, Technical Study **17** gives information on court markings and equipment. Volume 3 should be referred to particularly regarding outdoor surfaces. Other Technical Studies of the Handbook are referred to in the individual Data Sheets.

2 Sports for the disabled

There are very few sports not played at all by disabled people, but some sports cannot be played by people with certain disabilities.

Naturally, as far as practicable space dimensions are the same as the standards given in the table for each Data Sheet.

However, a few modifications are necessary, for example for siting basketball. Where space standards differ for disabled play, dimensions are given in the right-hand column of the table beneath the symbol.

A comprehensive handbook on provision for disabled people in sports and recreation facilities is being prepared by the Disabled Living Foundation and the Sports Council, to be published by the Architectural Press. It will include dimensions for sports for the disabled, including special and adapted activities.

The International Stoke Mandeville Federation publishes handbooks for the sports which are included in the International Stoke Mandeville Games (the Olympics of the Paralysed) held in each Olympic Year.

3 Metrication

In the UK the governing bodies of the sports listed below still require their playing area dimensions to be published, and to be marked out, in the original imperial notation.

To readily identify the sports concerned, and to acknowledge their prerogative, on the individual sports Data Sheets their imperial dimensions are given in brackets following the metric conversion required for the design and building of facilities.

Indoor sports: Archery (15 and 20yd ranges besides metric ones), rackets, real tennis.

Outdoor sports: Archery, baseball, croquet, crown green bowling, american football, association football (but FIFA publish metric dimensions), hockey, polo, shinty.

By far the majority of governing bodies now publish and mark-out using metric dimensions. Some have 'rounded-off' dimensions; others have converted exactly. Most still give the old imperial equivalent for the benefit of ground staff and officials who are as yet not conversant with metrication.

A few sports, such as rugby union football, have been faced with rephrasing traditionally known features of the pitch: for example the 'twenty-five' (yard line) has had to be renamed the 'twenty-two metre line' to avoid distorting the proportions of the midfield area; the 10 yard line, however, remains the 10m line.

4 Further information

An updated directory and guide to governing bodies of sport is available from the Sports Council's Information Centre.

Part I Indoor
common space
activities

1
Aikido

Aikido is a competitive combat sport, and one of the 'martial arts', based on an ancient Japanese system of self-defence. Force is not met with counter-force but with avoiding action, enabling the defender to take advantage of the attacker's temporary loss of balance to score with a successful aikido technique.

Siting
The mat can be placed anywhere in a common sports space, a practice hall or large projectile hall, having a minimum clear area of at least 9 × 9m preferably with a surrounding safety area, with a minimum clear height of 3·0m, **2**.
For competitions at least three combat areas are required in a minimum overall space of 33 × 13m.

Space

| | Standard of combat | | |
	N	C	R
Combat mat	9 × 9m	9 × 9m	9 × 9m
Minimum safety area around	1·5m	1·0m	1·0m
Additional officials' table margin: one side	+ 1·0m min	+ 1·0m min	—
Minimum overall area	13 × 12m	12 × 11m	11 × 11m

Floor mats
Consult specialist equipment suppliers. Sectional mats must be prevented from slipping or opening-up.
The MAC suggests that preferably a 'soft floor', without need for mats, should be considered for the various martial arts. This could be particularly suited to practice halls or specialist training and combat rooms where other activities such as gymnastics and movement and dance would also benefit from the surface resilience.

Surrounding enclosure
Hall walls or netting. In small practice halls, walls should be padded by upstanding mats or mattresses to a minimum height of 1m.

Internal environment
As for Judo.

Competitors and judges
Allow changing space for 5 persons per contest.

Spectators
Some mat-side chairs can be arranged in the spaces on both sides of the officials table or on tiered units around the safety area. Spectators should be at least 1·5–2m from the mat depending on the standard of competition. The sport is developing and could possibly attract 1000 or more spectators and devotees at major events and championships.

Storage
Storage will be required for mats on trolleys, officials' table and scoreboards.

Critical factors
For this bare-footed sport the floor surface, cleanliness and personal hygiene are important. Flush walls, and safety padding where necessary.

Source of reference
The Martial Arts Commission

1 *Photo: Colorsport*

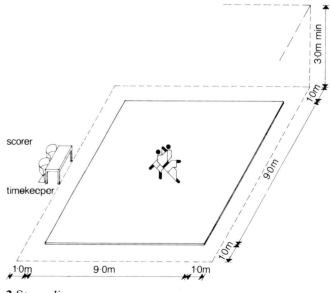

2 *Space diagram*

2

2
Archery

See also Volume 2, Part II, Technical Study **6**.

Space
The general layout of an indoor range is shown in **2**.
The official distances of Rounds are:
- At 15 yds Club and Recreational
- At 18m at a 400mm diam target face
- At 20 yds (18·29m) at a 16in (406mm) diam target face
- At 25m at a 600mm diam target face
- At 30m at an 800mm diam target face
- 3 competitors to each
- Target stand at a minimum of 914mm intervals while shooting (competition rules)

Walls and safety nets
Where a passageway is necessary for other users of the hall (best to avoid this if possible) or where simultaneous use of adjacent hall space is unavoidable, provide a continuous safety screen of white archery mesh, or stop netting between other activities. A tackle box shelf measuring 750 × 300 × 75mm is an advantage in the zone behind the shooting line.

Source of reference
Grand National Archery Society and 1977 Rules of Shooting: Part XI.

1 *Photo: Grand National Archery Society*

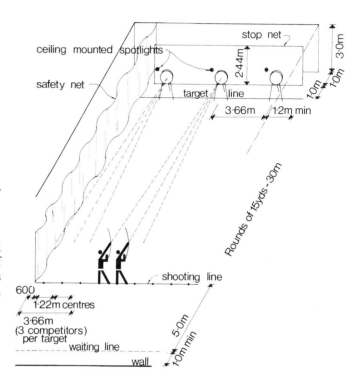

2 *Diagrammatic setting out of targets and archers for the various recognised lengths of Rounds*

3
Badminton

Siting

This is the indoor sport in greatest demand and with the smallest court size: at least two or three fitting into the smallest of the sports hall (sizes recommended in Table II, Vol 2, pp 46–7) and up to eight courts of top-class play standards in large ('two-court') halls, **2, 3**.

Space

	Standard of play		
	N	C†	R
Playing area (doubles court)			
Length	13·4m	13·4m	
Width	6·1m	6·1m	
Wall from base-line	2·25m	1·52m min	as for C
Wall from side line*	2·22m	1·22m min	
Between parallel courts	1·98m*	0·91m min	
Overall area			
For a single court	17·9 × 10·54m	16·44 × 8·54m min	
For a parallel pair	17·9 × 18·62m	16·44 × 15·55m* min	
For each additional court	+ min 8·08m	7·01m min (excluding side wall space allowed within a parallel pair*)	
Height see also 'Height of Hall' below	9·14m	7·62m	6·7–7·6m

* Where halls are subdivided by netting, a full side margin of 1·22m should be allowed along both sides of the net when setting out adjacent badminton courts, as shown in **3**.
† The Badminton Association of England advise that international and county players both require a height clearance of 9·14m.

In a multi-purpose sports hall where other games may be programmed to take place at the same time as badminton, there are usually conflicting demands of compatibility to be resolved by the management. Basketball and volleyball, for example, are noisy and will disturb even recreational badminton play. Tennis, table tennis (providing netting is drawn between the two spaces to stop balls running into the badminton courts), fencing and judo are satisfactory simultaneous activities.

However, distraction caused by lights, movement and noise, can be largely overcome by curtains or netting drawn between different activity zones, and at the back of courts where these are not near walls, **5**. Curtains will screen lights and movement, and deaden noise.

The Badminton Association of England recommends that the entrance to the hall should be at the side and not at the back of a court, so that people using it do not distract players. This applies particularly to multi-court halls, but in small halls where courts are placed across its width, it is more difficult to avoid doorways in side walls along the ends of courts.

Building conversions

When considering the increasingly frequent question of redundant building conversions for sport, the critical factors to be examined for recreational badminton include clear heights and the shape of the ceiling, the floor space, lighting and background.

Some compromises inevitably will become acceptable, as has

1 *Badminton between the beams at Belgrave Centre, Tamworth. The fluorescent light fittings are protected by translucent covers and mounted each side of the roof beams, situated over the space between courts. Note that the light fittings for other sports are placed on the diagonal ties and shielded to prevent glare, if left on, when high service lobs are played. Photo: David Butler*

been the case for so long where badminton is played in local, often cramped social halls:

Height: Any obstruction (such as roof structure or light fittings) is undesireable but those along the length of the court are likely to be less serious than those across it. If possible, courts should be arranged to fit between beams on to which side lighting can be mounted, **1, 6**. For childrens' and recreational play the acceptable minimum clear height could be in the region of 5·4–6·1m, with the hope of more height between the existing structure and beneath a pitched roof.

Shape: In long narrow halls the measurements may dictate an end-to-end court location, where it is then desirable to divide the courts with a curtain or blinkered sportnet, allowing on

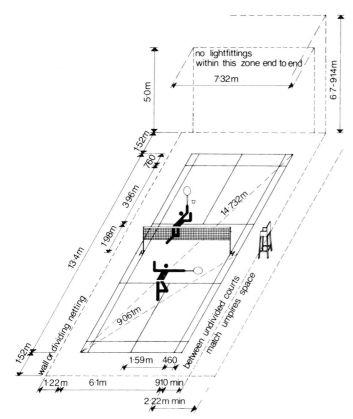

2 *Diagram of badminton space. See also* **6**, *showing badminton zone height rationally taken to underside of purlins. Dimensions for the standards of play are given in the table. Note the reduced minimum space between parallel undivided courts and the minimum space one side for an umpire's chair*

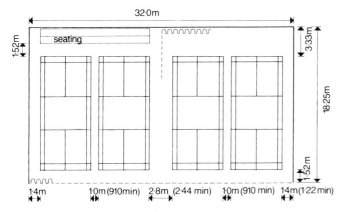

3 *Suggested setting out of pairs of courts in a 36·5 × 32m large hall to allow for space dividing nets and some spectator/players' seating. Courts should be parallel but if end to end, then sight-screens,* **5**, *should be hung between the end of courts. For a small hall flexible layout, see Volume 2 page 50, showing a triple group of badminton courts and volleyball court sited together*

both sides an absolute minimum baseline distance of 0·76m, but preferably 1·5m. Side margins could be reduced to an absolute minimum of 0·91m. These margin reductions could also apply in wider spaces where it is just possible to place courts across the hall. The minimum space for recreational badminton in such cramped conditions seems to be 15 × 7m, subject to the position of doorways and protrusions.

Floor: The problems likely to need attention are worn and uneven surfaces, and distorted timber floors. Consult TUS for further advice.

4 *Roll-down mat court showing the storage roller. Manufacturers' sizes should be checked against the required overall area given in the table of dimensions. Photo: En-tout-Cas Limited*

Height of halls

The Badminton Association of England, as the governing body of the sport in England, believes that 6·7m (quoted as suitable for recreational play throughout this book) is an unacceptable height for badminton since it will discourage the development of a full range of shots. A height of 6·7m certainly is not acceptable for national or county competitions organised by the Association and may not be acceptable for some local league play nor for coaching.

The Sports Council maintains that a height of 6·7m to 7·6m would be acceptable for recreational play. A 1977/8 research project has suggested that shuttles are rarely hit above 6·7m even in club play and the highest point of flight is not over the net, as implied in the Badminton Association of England handbook, but approximately halfway between the net and the rear service line. From this the Sports Council would conclude that 6·7m is adequate for recreational play, but that 7·6m is necessary for club competitions and coaching.

The Badminton Association of England would dispute this view and states in its 1979/80 handbook: 'Halls of less than 7·6m from the floor at a point over the net are unsuitable for the game to be played to a reasonable standard'. The full findings of the research study are to be published by the Sports Council in a research working paper.

The definition of 'recreational standard' for badminton given in the Table should therefore be 'play on a non-competitive basis including "friendly" matches where players will amicably agree to what constitutes a "let" should the shuttlecock be obstructed by an impediment in height'. Most local leagues play a 'let' if the shuttlecock hits any projections below the roof and a 'fault' if it hits the roof itself.

The Scottish Badminton Union endorse the view that less than 7·6m is unsuitable, even for recreation play, and stress the needs of coaching, and for singles play requiring more height. The SBU suggest that most height is needed close to the rear of court and not over the net, or in mid-court. Uniformity of height, clear of beams, net tracks and other fixed equipment is also stressed.

See also added height notes with illustrations **2** and **6**.

Spectators

This sport has developed as a major spectator attraction in recent years and now attracts television coverage to its major event, the All-England Championships, and to other events. The BAoE consider that in all halls providing first-class facilities, plenty of space for spectators is a necessity. In large halls at least 18m is recommended between walls in the lengthways direction of the court. This leaves space at each end for two rows of spectators and chairs for players between games (see **3**). In the other extreme, the potential capacity at major events is estimated at 5000 plus.

For tournaments and 'centre-court' matches spectator accommodation is normally in the form of mobile seating

5a *Ideally, in multi-sports halls, sight-screen curtains should match the background colour, to avoid sudden contrasts of background which increases the difficulty to follow a fast moving shuttle across the sight-screen height. Manufacturers offer a limited range of screens and dark green is a conventional, but often sharply contrasting, colour. The preferred height for the solid sight-screen should be carefully considered and may vary for differing standards of play. Curtains are attached to the sportsnets. Any added weight must be allowed for in the suspension system. Photo: Gillinson Barnett & Partners*

units wheeled into any position required at the same level as the players.

Floor and court markings
(See also Volume 2, Part II, Technical Study **17**).
The floor may be of wood, composition or plastic materials, but it must not be slippery. The finish should be dull to avoid reflected light which adds to the difficulty of sighting the shuttle. The Scottish Badminton Union say that some 'give' in the floor surface is desirable to prevent injuries.
Regulation court markings are matt finish white lines 38mm wide *included* within overall dimensions of court. Yellow is recommended for recreational standard courts (but see Handball).
Roll-down mat courts are also available as shown in **4**. Roll down PVC and other sheeting has been tried out but problems experienced include rucking and the rolled weight. Special storage rollers can be supplied to ease storage and removal. The size of roll down courts should be checked against the overall area given in the table above, particularly the length. A change of surface level within the minimum space should be avoided if possible.

b

c

5b, c *Shuttle is clearly seen against dark walls, but above it can be lost against sharply contrasting ceiling and* brightness *of natural top light. Photos: b Spurgeon Walker Associates Ltd, c Stewart Clark*

Walls

A suitable background against which a fast-moving shuttle can be seen easily is most important. Badminton requires a hall with four plain walls with no windows or glass. If viewing windows are necessary in walls at court ends, then curtains or blinds must be fitted to avoid distracting match players. For top standards of play, games nets and other distracting attachments should be removable.

The back walls should be finished in medium-to-dark shades with a matt surface. For reflectance values see *IES Lighting guide: Sports*, pp 21, 22. A gloss finish reflects the light. This applies equally to the side walls, as many shots are played to the side of the body looking towards the side of the court. Walls at opposite ends of court should be identical. The colour of walls is discussed in TUS Data Sheet 2.5. The use of sight screen curtains has been mentioned in 'Siting' above. Related problems are shown in **5a–c**.

Avoid all ledges which will trap shuttles—see **10a** and **10b** on p 147 in Volume 2. Practice basketball backboards behind a court should be removable.

Lighting

Players must be able to follow the flight of the shuttlecock against the background and do so without being troubled by glare or having their attention distracted by bright light sources near their sight lines. The shuttlecock is seen by light transmitted by, and reflected from, the translucent 'feathers'. Natural lighting, if any, should be confined to roof lights positioned and manufactured to give even lighting and free from glare and sun penetration. See Volume 2, Part II, Technical Study **16**.

Three basic methods of artificial lighting, **6**, are used depending upon the permanency of badminton use, the degree of multi-purpose use in the hall and the standard of play being designed for:

- **Removable lighting:** Temporary portable low-brightness luminaires placed on stands at each end of the net
- **Drop-down lighting:** Similar, but suspended on lowering gear. Supplementary circuits to allow main lighting to be dimmed or switched off for badminton match play
- **Fixed lighting:** Also supplementary circuits. Angle reflectors or diffusing luminaires are suitable, mounted on wall or ceiling at a minimum height of 5m

In *multi-purpose halls* it is important that:

- Background lighting over the courts can be turned off to avoid players suffering blank sighting spots and glare
- Lights left on in other areas are screened from players view (see Siting)
- Supplementary purpose-designed lighting for badminton is provided for each court related to the spaces between courts. The use of a desynchronisation pulse unit to fluorescent lights could be used but is not essential
- Adequately lighting the back of the service court area should also be considered to give overall even lighting in the back area where the high service lob drops. Any lights so placed across the court should be separately switched and screened on the net side to avoid glare to the server at the opposite end (see **6** and **7**).

For essential detailed advice, refer to:

- *BAoE (annual) Handbook: conditions and technical data*
- TUS Data Sheet 2.5 *Lighting in Sports Halls*: Tamworth development projects 6 and 7
- *IES Guide: lighting for sport*
- Lighting for television: see Volume 1, Technical Study **19**, p 117 and consult TV companies' lighting plans

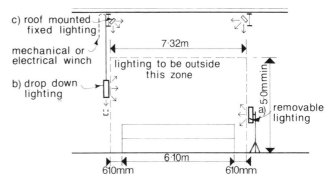

6 *Diagram showing various methods of artificial lighting*
(a) *portable illumination tends to give fall-off towards the back of court*
(b) *low brightness luminaires at both ends of the net; or for multi-purpose halls, two 1·8m strip lights both sides of the court spaced apart as shown on 7*
(c) *where the roof beams are outside the badminton court, 1, the required clear heights (see table) can be taken to the underside of secondary structure or flush ceiling. (Minimum clear height for other sports beneath the main beam is 7·0m.)*

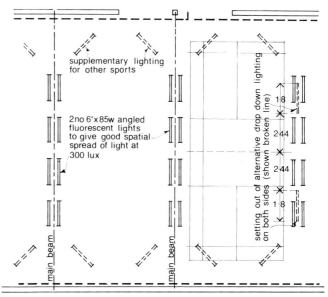

7 *Lighting layout at the TUS development project 1 at Tamworth. Ideally the badminton zone should be 'up-lit'. The IES type of illuminaire up-lighters rely to some extent on a low surface brightness to prevent uncomfortable glare for players. In multi-sports halls, such as Tamworth, where the fittings are at high level, care must be taken in positioning them outside the play zone and as far as possible from the end walls. Light fittings should be positioned so that the shuttle cock does not 'track' in front of them during play. Again, a low surface brightness will reduce uncomfortable glare. The layout also shows the alternative drop-down fluorescent light arrangements suggested by The Badminton Association of England for multi-purpose halls*

Heating and ventilation

Any temperature above 50°F (10°C) makes conditions unpleasant for the players, but some increase may be desirable for spectator events in the interest of their comfort. Warmer air can also affect the flight of plastic shuttles. For this reason, as with natural feathers, different speeds of shuttle are available to suit the temperatures of the playing hall.

Any air-conditioning system which moves the air can deflect the shuttlecock. A draught-free atmosphere is essential (see fig **18**, p 148, Volume 2).

Equipment

When the court is permanently in use for badminton, the most satisfactory and convenient net posts are those with a metal base which can be screwed to the floor on the side lines. Where this is not possible posts with well-weighted bases which will hold the net taut at its correct height can be obtained (see **8**).

Apart from a few rackets kept at the hall for beginners, users are encouraged to buy their own equipment. For this purpose a shop could be considered as part of the ancillary accommodation, positioned in the entrance hall.

Storage

Storage space close to the courts is required for posts and nets. As the posts are extremely heavy, trolleys are employed for easier movement when setting up apparatus. Two trolleys occupying a space 3m × 3m accommodate all the apparatus required by four badminton courts.

Changing

For the method of assessing the number of players to be accommodated see Volume 2, Part II, Technical Study **11**. Adequate showers and locker provision for peak court change over times are considered important.

Critical considerations

Adequate height and lighting over *all* the court/plain background colour to contrast with shuttle/glare-free side lighting/avoidance of shuttle trap ledges on walls and in roof structure/special lighting circuits/type and location of heater/vent units.

Sources of information

BAoE Annual *Handbook: halls for badminton, conditions and technical data*
TUS Development Project: Belgrave Centre Sports Hall, Tamworth, Staffordshire
Governing bodies of sport for badminton

8 *Well-weighted net posts. Photo: Powersport International and Unit 17*

4
Basketball and mini-basketball

Siting

Provided the court has a minimum margin of extra space around it, including match officials' table and team benches, this game can be played in a common hall space, **3**.

Space

	Standards of play			
	⊛ N	C	R	♿
Playing area				
Length*	26·0m	26·0m	do	
Width*	14·0m	14·0m	do	
Clear area around	min 1·0m**	min 1·0m**	do	†
Officials and teams' one side	+ 1·3m	+ 1·3m		†
Overall area	26–30m × 16·3–18·3m**	26–30m × 16·3–18·3m**	min 26 × 15m	
Height minimum	7·0m	7·0m	6·7m	

* Court measurements can be adjusted as follows: ±2m on the length and ±1m on the width: *the variations being proportional to each other*.
** Increase on other side and at ends if spectator seating is to be provided: the governing bodies recommend that spectators should be at least 2m from the court.
† It is advisable to increase margin widths to at least 1·5m to allow wheel-chairs to pivot back into court.

In order to ensure that substitution is carried out efficiently the arrangement of team benches and substitute benches/chairs shown on the axonometric diagram is recommended. This arrangement is obligatory for all matches. The officials seated at the table must be able to see the court clearly. The benches and chairs for substitutes must therefore be lower than the chairs for the officials, or alternatively the officials' table and chairs be placed on a platform, if spectator sight-lines allow (see **39b** on p 107 in Volume 2).

Court markings

Court dimensions are *exclusive* of the 50mm-wide perimeter lines. In the case of courts for top-level competition in halls with a variety of other sports markings, it is desirable for the side-lines and end-lines to be marked with wider tape, eg 100mm. For details of court markings see Volume 1, Part IV, Technical Study **17**. It should be noted that for standards of play N and C the recommended colour is black and that for standard of play R the recommended colour is dark blue. However, the Amateur Basketball Association of Scotland advise white or brightly coloured markings. See also 'Floor'

1 *A capacity audience of 1600 watched the 1979 Butlins' Men's National Cup Final held at Concord Sports Centre, Sheffield. Photo: English Basket Ball Association*

2 *Women's League basketball is increasing in demand and is rivalling the widespread men's leagues as a major indoor spectator sport. Tigers V Corvus, Dacorum Leisure Centre 1979. Photo: James Dunlop*

3a *Space diagram. Note that match courts must be set out with a wider space along one side for match tables and team benches. For top level play place table on a 300mm raised platform. In shorter sports halls and courts, specify side folding basketball goal units suspend 1·0–2·5m off the rear wall (in increments of 300mm). The board face must always be 1·2m inside the rear line. In longer halls increments up to 5m projections from rear walls are possible. Side wall practice goals should also fold. Hand or electric winch operated backboards are shown in Badminton photograph 5b on p 6. Other varieties include a forward fold unit and fully electrically operated types, forward or backfold. These are particularly suitable, if roof loadings allow, for the centre court situation in large or multi purpose halls and in arenas*

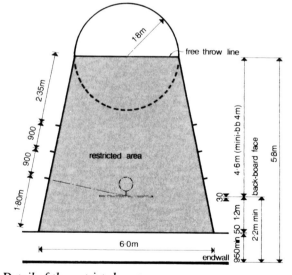

* dimensions taken from inside of boundary lines

below regarding markings on roll-down removable playing surfaces.

Spectator facilities
It is desirable that spectators are at least 2·0m distant from the court. Best viewing is from the sides as the solid backboards at each end tend to obstruct the view. This is a spectator growth sport, and potentially could increase its attraction as standards continue to improve. The England Basketball Association advise that a minimum of 250 spectators should be allowed for all standards of play. For National League matches a minimum of 1,500 seats is required. For major national and European events, the potential capacity is now estimated at 8000 plus.

Floor
Flooring should be slip resistant and non-splinter. Ball to surface resilience is also important, (see Volume 2, Part II Technical Study **17**).
Note the toned 'restricted area', shown on **3**, which is coloured to contrast with the surrounding floor. Anchor sockets are required for mobile backboard/goal units, **4**.
Roll-down 30 × 15m portable courts are available to order (see also Volume 2, p 142).
Recent developments include a 'carpet' material used for the 1980 national final. This proved successful with the teams and particularly comfortable for players with leg troubles who, it is claimed, might not otherwise have lasted out the full time.
Also, a lineless portable court is being developed for coloured television presentations. It uses attractive, contrasting colours for the court, the restricted area, the semi-circles and the out-of-court surrounds: where the joint is the inside mea-

3b *Detail of the restricted area*

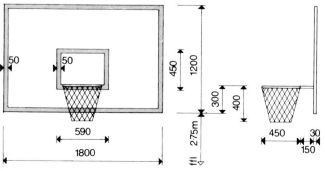

3c *Detail of the basket board*

surement of the court and becomes the foot-foul 'line'. For further details of both consult TUS.

Surrounding surfaces or enclosure
(See also Volume 2, Part II, Technical Studies **16** and **18**). The walls or roof structure should be capable of supporting a heavy backboard at both ends. The method of support should be identical, ie both ceiling-hung or both wall-hung as shown in **3**. Consult suppliers for loadings and fixings. Practice goals can be mounted along side walls clear of doorways. Consider the wall colour as a means of providing contrast to backboards which are painted white (or are transparent plyglass). Consider the height of flush walls (clear of projections) also required for handball and micro-korfball etc.

Technical equipment
● Scoreboard capable of recording scores of two teams, up to 199–199, **5**.
● Stop/start clock capable of recording passing of time in seconds. If possible, it requires a count-down mechanism with a preset facility. Power lead
● Two loud sounding devices, distinct from each other

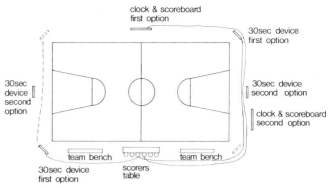

4 *Mobile folding backboard goal units particularly suitable in large halls or arena for setting out a centre court. Available with integral weighted base, or anchored by floor sockets. With floor mounted types all supports and framework below height of 2·75m must be a minimum of 1m behind the end line. Photo: Powersport International Limited*

5 *English Basketball Association's layout for technical control equipment*

should be incorporated in the scoreboard/clock (NB from experience, these devices are invariably found to be not loud enough). One of these devices should sound automatically in the case of a count-down clock reaching zero. They should both also have the facility to be operated manually.
● It is desirable for the timekeeper to have a separate control panel from that of the scoreboard operator, **5**.
● 'Thirty seconds' alarms are required, one at each end of the court, to be operated from the scorer's table. These should have a sounding device distinct from the scoreboard sounds. For major matches four alarms may be required, **5**.
● All technical equipment must be operable from the scorer's table. This must be situated just off the court, opposite the halfway line, **3** and **5**.
● The scoreboard and clock should be situated in such a manner that they can be easily seen by the officials sitting at the scorer's table (see below), the players, coaches, and spectators

Internal environment
● Background heating min of 12·8°C is required for players and for *substitutes* to be able to sit for long periods in conditions which enable them to perform precision skills immediately upon entering the game
● Mechanical ventilation is best, providing a maximum of 4 air changes an hour
● Natural light from above. Artificial lighting should be robust and protected from impact (see the *IES Guide*, p 23)
● The game is noisy and should not be played at the same time as less noisy activities such as badminton. Walls and ceilings should be designed to reduce reverberation.

Storage
If backboards cannot be suspended, storage space is required for two portable (and preferable folding) goal units as shown in **4** and **6**. Match official tables and the time-keeping and scoring equipment listed above will also require storage.

Critical factors
Siting and space for officials and teams/type of backboard support system/match control equipment/minimum temperature/noise control/high quality portable floor surface in arenas, or for top-standard matches/mobile goal units must be fully padded, and fully anchored to prevent any movement and to ensure rigidity of the goal.

Basketball outdoors
The English Basketball Association, with financial support from the Sports Council, is campaigning to promote outdoor casual play areas in order to widen the game's popularity. The pitch is similar to that used for indoor basketball and further information is obtainable from the governing bodies.

6 *Folded-down goal: allow a storage space of 3m long ×
1·85m × 2m high*

Mini-basketball

The size of the court is now 18 × 10·5m to 26 × 14m. Other
court markings are also the same as for basketball, except
that backboards are placed only 4m from the free-throw
lines. In small halls, other variable measurements can be
used providing these are in the same proportion to one
another.

The main significant differences between mini-basketball
and the parent sport are the reduced size of backboards and
height of the basket above the floor, **7, 8**, and the reduced
free-throw distance.

Source of reference
Governing bodies of sport
Manufacturers' of sports equipment

7 *Mobile goals can be set at mini-basketball height. Otherwise,
junior basketball can be played across the hall using side-wall
practice boards at senior height*

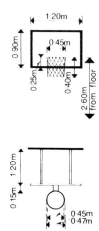

8 *Mini-Basketball backboard and goal dimensions*

5
Bowling: the short mat game

The game is highly developed in Ireland. There are over 800 affiliated clubs scattered throughout Northern Ireland and a small number in the Republic of Ireland clustered in Dublin, Cork and Co. Donegal. In Wales the game is known as Short-Greens Bowls.

The game is enjoyed by both men and women of all ages and there are opportunities to play at club level, in league and open competitions and in the National Championships.

Siting
Most clubs play in church halls, works and recreation club premises, community halls and leisure centres. A recommended floor space for clubs is 18·3 × 10·7m which will allow play on three mats with an adequate surround for spectators. A space as small as 13·7 × 3·66m would be sufficient for one mat. In Wales a rink space is 13·7–25m long by 3–5m wide.

Floor surface
The surface should be level and may be of wood strip, wood block, concrete, composition or synthetic materials. Uneven floors may be corrected by using hardboard sheets underneath the mat.

The rink mat
The mat, **2**, consists of green felt or other approved bowls surface with an underlay or, alternatively, an approved green material with bonded rubber or foam backing. The length is 12·2–13·7m × a width of 1·83m with a tolerance of 50mm. The markings on the mat should be made with 12·5mm white adhesive tape.

Lighting
For a three mat area the suggested level of illuminace is 250 lux. Twin 1·8m fluorescent fittings using warm white tubes are suitable. In a hall with a low ceiling the installation of a diffuser should be considered and where the ceiling height exceeds 4·57m metal reflectors are likely to be required on the fluorescent fittings.

Heating
An ambient temperature of 16°C in the hall is desirable.

Other equipment
Two rubber delivery mats each measuring 610 × 356mm are required for each green. Fenders and block can be made from 76mm square wood and they should be painted white. The 127mm diameter outdoor bowl is the most common choice. Sixteen bowls, preferably divided into two different colours, are required for each mat. The jack is the same as that used in the outdoor game except that a heavier ·42kg jack is recommended for bonded mats. The Welsh game also uses a heavier indoor jack.

Source of reference and essential further advice
Sports Council of Northern Ireland Advisory leaflet No. 7
The Irish and Welsh governing bodies of sport

1 *National indoor short mat bowling championships at Antrim Forum. Photo: The Sports Council for Northern Ireland*

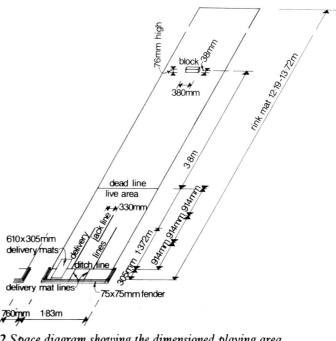

2 *Space diagram showing the dimensioned playing area*

6
Boxing

Siting

Boxing may take place in a common sports space or specialist boxing club facility. Contests are boxed on a raised ring, **2**, whereas recreational boxing, coaching and training usually take place at floor level. See also Volume 2, Part II, Technical Study **5** for boxing club use of practice halls and weight-training rooms.

Space

Ring area	Standards of play			
	⚬⚬	N	C	R
Inside ropes	6·0m sq	4·90–6·10m sq	3·66–6·10m sq	min 3·66m sq
Outer ring around	0·500m	0·5m	0·5m	0·5m
Ringside clearance around for officials (and press seats)	5·0m	min 2·0m	min 2·0m	2·0m circulation
Overall area	17m sq (see fig 3)	9·9–11·1m sq	8·66–11·1m sq	min 8·66m sq
Floor-to-ceiling height (suggested)	—	min 6·7m*	min 4·5m	min 3·5m

* 7·6m where TV lighting luminaires to be mounted at approximately 6·7m height above floor

Spectators

Viewing is from all around, both at floor level and from surrounding stepped seating (see Volume 1, Part IV, Technical Study **12**). The potential crowd capacity required at major events is estimated at up to 10 000.

Floor

For boxing training at floor level, this should be preferably wood strip covered with a 15–19mm thick mat of felt, foam rubber or other suitable approved material (having the same elasticity), topped with stretched canvas. If a raised platform is not used, a means of anchoring the corner posts which support the ropes must be provided. Fixing may be also required for mounting a punch ball and bag for boxing training.

Internal environment

- Background heating of only 10°–12·8°C is required for boxers, but if spectators are present a higher level (at least 15·0°C) will be required.
- When considering ventilation, it should be noted that good mechanical inlet and extract to counter heat from concentrated lighting will be required.
- Separate, localised lighting is required. Rings are usually lit in one of two ways: by an overhead lighting system or a floodlighting system

Overhead lighting system

Luminaires which concentrate most of the light downwards are suspended over the ring and surrounded by shields to restrict glare. This system is shown as A in **4**. Although illuminances on the horizontal are high, the corresponding values on the vertical are relatively low and distant spectators may find it difficult to follow the action.

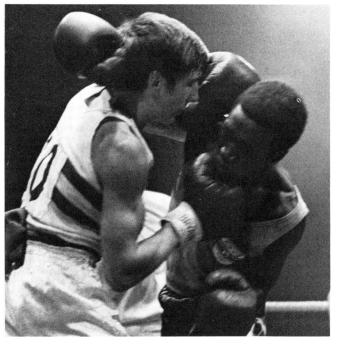

1 *Photo: CPNA*

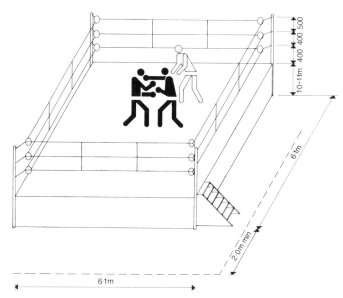

2 *Most contests are held in a three-roped ring, though amateur bouts may be held in a two-roped ring*

A modified overhead system is often used when boxing to club or recreational standards takes place in a multi-purpose sports hall. The general lighting should then be supplemented by local lighting over the ring. In a typical arrangement nine 1500W tungsten halogen floodlights are carried on a 4m × 4m tubular steel frame fitted with raising

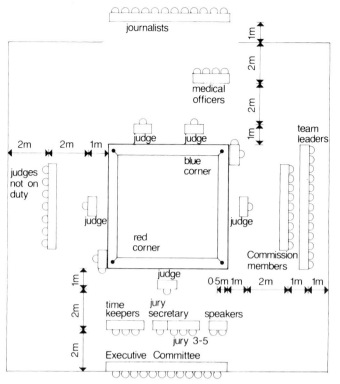

3 *Dimensions for Olympic, European and World Championship ringside space*

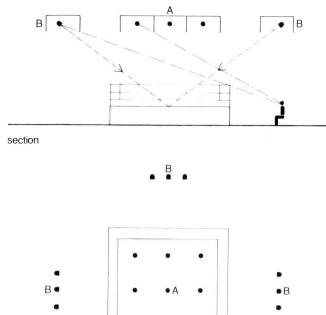

4 *Layout of boxing floodlights*

Standard of match	Service illuminance lux	Plane of measurement	Luminaire data		
			BZ classification*	Flux fraction ratio*	Mounting height m
N	2000	Horizontal on floor of ring	BZ2	0	5 (minimum)
C	1000	,,	,,	,,	,, ,,
R	300	,,	,,	,,	,, ,,

* See manufacturers' data

and lowering gear. The frame incorporates baffles to restrict the spill light and a microphone socket, and is lowered into position when required.

An illuminance of about 2000 lux on the horizontal over a 6m × 6m ring is provided by nine 1500W tungsten filament lamps, or 400W high pressure discharge lamps, in concentrating reflectors mounted 6m above the ring and spaced as shown at **A** in **4**.

Floodlighting system

In the second system, which is preferable but calls for more design skill, floodlights are grouped on each side of the ring at some distance from it (**B** in **4**), and aimed towards its centre. The lower the mounting height, the higher will be the illuminance on vertical surfaces within the ring, but the greater will be the risk of severe glare to front spectators. A satisfactory compromise is achieved by positioning the floodlights at an angle of about 45° from the centre of the ring. External glare shields can be used to restrict spill light.

As an example, an illuminance of about 1000 lux is provided

on vertical planes over a 6 × 6m ring by groups of three floodlights on each side of the ring, as shown at **B** in **4**. Each floodlight is equipped with a 1500W tungsten halogen lamp, or a 400W high pressure discharge lamp.

Noise control is not a problem, except at spectator events.

Equipment

Standards of design and manufacture are laid down in *BS 1892: Gymnasium equipment. 1972.*

Storage

Storage is required for corner posts, ropes and floor mat, and complete demountable rings.

Critical considerations

Lighting for tournaments/ventilation.

Source of reference

Amateur Boxing Association

Standard of match	Service illuminance lux	Plane of measurement	Aiming point	Floodlight data		
				Beam classification	Type	Mounting height m
N	1000	Vertical, 1m above floor of ring	Ring centre	1–2 or H5 V2–3	A, B or C	5 (minimum)
C	500	,,	,,	,,	,,	,, ,,
R	150	,,	,,	,,	,,	,, ,,

7
Cricket

Six-a-side game

The indoor game has developed with the increase in indoor sports centres and a national knock-out competition exists for clubs, **1**. There is a potential for this to be extended to counties which might be very popular. The indoor two-wicket international competition held at Wembley Arena may be indicative of the greater promotion and professionalism coming in to the game which may create significant development. The spectator potential is not known at this stage.

Space

Playing area	Six-a-side game maximum	minimum
Length	**36·5m**	30·4m
Width	27·4–30·4m	18·30m
Height	7·6m	6·10m
Width of lines	25cm	

1 *Six-a-side in Enfield Grammar School sports hall. Photo: Enfield Gazette*

Surrounding surfaces and enclosure
As for cricket practice, but space must be allowed for wicket dividing nets, which are not in use, to be drawn back across the bowler's end, **2**.

Special requirements
Spectators should be confined to the bowler's end or in a two-court hall, should view the game through netting along one side. Otherwise, requirements are as for practice.

Net practice

When siting cricket practice there are three similar situations:
- In a sports hall **3, 4, 5**
- In a projectile hall (see Volume 2, Part II, Technical Study **6**)
- In a specially designed indoor Cricket School (see below)

Flooring
In most cases cricket is accommodated within the sports hall using practice nets with portable roll-out strips. These are made of rubber and plastics similar to the thick sheet variety described in Volume 2, Part II, Technical Study **17**, but also include a short-pile version of artificial grass. For further details and products consult the Sports Council Information Centre and TUS.
For other elemental details see Volume 2, Part II, Technical Study **6**

Cricket schools

Although cricket schools are purpose-designed enclosures, managers are finding it an economic necessity to use the large space for other compatible activities and sports such as badminton, volleyball, combat sports, keep-fit, local gatherings and even as refreshment areas on outdoor big-match days. Cricket schools should therefore be designed as multi-purpose areas compatible with cricket performance specifications, **6**.

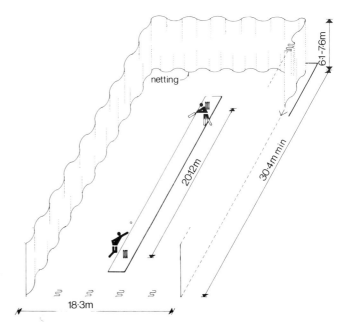

2 *Diagram of six-a-side cricket space. See also table of dimensions*

To avoid distraction to batsmen, court markings for other sports must be confined to the 'bowler's end' and not over-marked on the built-in synthetic wickets. Roll-down overlay courts could be used over mid-wicket areas, but the exposed wickets should be protected when in other use.

Flooring
Where a special hall is provided for net practice or 6-a-side cricket, it is essential that the wicket should perform well in terms of rebound resilience (ball/surface), stiffness, friction, spin, resistance to set and wear. See also Volume 2, Technical Study **17**. For further advice on range of artificial indoor surfaces for cricket consult the Sports Council.

3 *Mixed cricket practice with portable roll up mats. Tracking fixed to roof structure can compel a costly height of netting. Photo: John Starling*

5 *White canvas blinker sheets are fixed to the netting for a length of 4·5m. Preferably, blinkers should be 1·8m high. Photo: Sports Council for Wales*

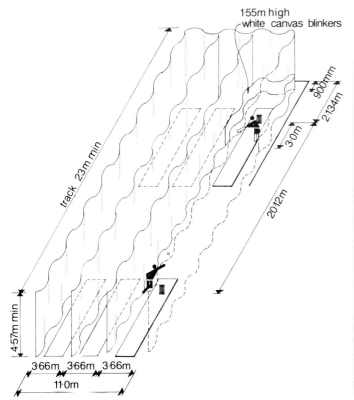

4 *Diagram of cricket practice nets. Note the minimum height of netting compared with the excessive height normal in halls of 6·7–9·1m height if tracking is fixed to the roof structure. Three nets require a space of 11m wide × 4·57m minimum height (6·7–9·1m actual) with as much length as possible (minimum 29·5m), in small halls it is important to position nets (1) in the badminton/volleyball zone to maintain flexible use of the end zone (behind bowler), and (2) along the far side wall to keep accessways clear*

6 *Indoor cricket school at Lords. The floor surface used in the nets has been designed to provide four 'fast' and three 'slow' lanes, while the overall dimensions and specifications of the hall will readily allow for the six-a-side game and a range of other sports. Ancillary accommodation includes changing space for 100, a viewing gallery with seating for 60, bar and restaurant, meeting room and a shop. Photo: Patric Eagar*

Other special requirements and sources of reference
Special requirements are generally as for those outlined in cricket practice in sports/projectile halls (see Volume 2, Technical Study **6**), but also consult the National Cricket Association (national coaches), and NCA publications *Indoor cricket* and *List of indoor facilities for cricket*. Nottinghamshire County Council Education Department also has publications on its own development of non-turf pitches. For lighting refer to the IES *Lighting Guide: Sport*.

17

8
Fencing

Siting

One of the advantages of fencing is that it can take place in any reasonably sized room or hall, provided that the lighting and the floor are suitable. Fencing lessons, training sessions, practice bouts and normal fencing (or loose play) should be provided for in surroundings which avoid distraction and interruption. However, as fencing competitions will probably be held in such spaces, it is desirable to base the dimensions on the area required for competitive pistes, **2**, using the table below.

Space

	Standards of play			
	⚭	N	C	R
Piste space				
Length	14m	14m	14m	14m
Width	1·8–2m	1·8–2m	1·8–2m	1·8–2m
Clear space both ends	1·5–2m	1·5–2m	1·5–2m	1·5–2m
Clear space both sides*	2·25–3m	2m	1·25–2m	1·25–2m
Space between parallel piste*		min 2·5m	min 2·5m	min 2·5m
Overall area				
Single piste		18 × 6m**	min 17 × 4·3m	as C
Two parallel piste	—	min 18 × 10·5m	min 17 × 8·6m	as C
Additional piste	—	+ 18 × 4·5m each	+ min 17 × 4·05 each	as C
Height	—	min 3·6m	min 3·6m	as C

* Including match officials' table space one side
** 18·0 × 8·0m for raised piste for final stages of World and Olympic tournaments

During a competition one piste will accommodate a pool of usually 6–8 competitors. A competition may start with several elimination pools, finishing with a final pool. Therefore, it is advisable to have as many marked-out regulation pistes as possible so that the maximum number of pools can be held simultaneously.

The minimum regulation piste total lengths will fit across the 17m width of small sports hall given in Table II on pp 46–7 in Volume 2.

Markings

When a metallic piste is not used, 50mm-wide white lines are marked out on to the floor surface, **3**.

Floor

It is important that the surface on which fencing takes place should be non-slip and impart a degree of person/surface resilience when in use. A wooden floor is ideal. When the floor is excessively slippery, or of a solid construction, a special roll-down rubber piste should be used. During fencing bouts using electronic scoring apparatus, a special metallic piste can be used. This prevents hits on the floor being registered by the electronic scoring apparatus. This is generally supplied as a roll of special mesh. When the floor is hard, a rubber piste can be laid directly beneath the metallic piste to minimise damage.

Provision must be made for attaching the mesh firmly in

1 *Photo: Sports Council Publications*

2 *Diagram of fencing piste showing officials' scoring table, equipment and spool cables*

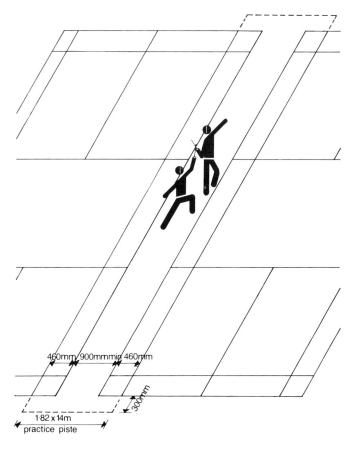

460mm 900mm min 460mm

300mm

1·82 x 14m
practice piste

3 *For fencing instruction white lines can be marked out across other games' coloured markings, or badminton tramlines used*

place during use. Normally the metallic piste is secured at each end using a standard straining device, held at the four corners of the piste by sockets set flush into the floor, **4**. If it is impossible to set inserts into the floor the strainers can be held by running chains to the wall. This becomes impractical if the hall is of a much greater length than the piste.

Alternatively, and particularly in the design of specialist fencing halls, sub-surface storage of the metallic piste and straining mechanism can be provided, **5**. The roll of metallic mesh is set in a pit at one end of the piste which when not in use is covered with a wooden trap-door. When in use the free end of the metallic piste is fastened by bolts into floor inserts **4**, or by chains to the wall. Straining is achieved by a winding mechanism incorporated within the pit.

For further details and advice about flooring overlays, straining mechanism and underfloor wiring, consult fencing equipment specialist suppliers.

Electronic scoring equipment and wiring

Today all but very elementary beginners fence competitively using electronic scoring apparatus. This consists of an electronic machine which is linked to the fencers by wires, and records both visually and audibly when a hit is scored. During the fencing bout each competitor is attached to a spring-loaded spool, which keeps the flexible cable from tailing on the ground as the fencer moves up and down the piste.

The electronic scoring apparatus is positioned on a table or specially designed trolley, placed at one side of the centre of the piste, **2** and **5**, and is wired to the spools.

There are two types of recording apparatus. One is a small compact club set which runs from a heavy-duty, dry-cell battery. This is used in practice and training sessions. It needs no external power source and is usually connected to

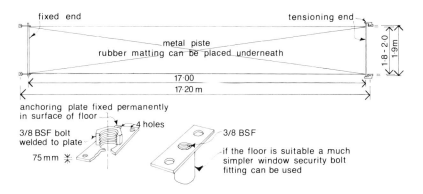

fixed end   tensioning end

metal piste
rubber matting can be placed underneath

1·8 - 2·0
1·9m

17·00
17·20 m

anchoring plate fixed permanently
in surface of floor
                              4 holes
3/8 BSF bolt   3/8 BSF
welded to plate
                                                         if the floor is suitable a much
75mm   simpler window security bolt
                                                         fitting can be used

4 *Layout for piste with surface straining mechanism. Leon Paul Equipment Limited*

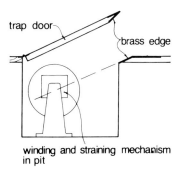

trap door
                    brass edge

winding and straining mechanism
in pit

5 *Layout for piste with sub surface connecting wiring, straining mechanism and storage pit. The leading edge of the storage pit*

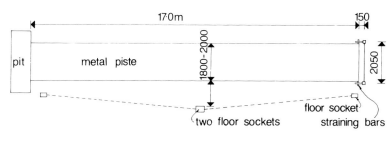

17·0m   150

1800-2000   2050

pit   metal piste

two floor sockets   floor socket
                                        straining bars

is bevelled to allow the trap door to close during fencing. Leon Paul Limited

19

the spools by free-running connecting cables. It is not normally used in conjunction with metallic pistes. The other type of apparatus is a more comprehensive and complex electronic recording set used in official, national and international events. It must conform to the Federation Internationale d'Escrime (FIE) regulations. This equipment requires the provision of a 13 amp outlet fused and earthed power socket, or a 12 volt accumulator (car-type), which should be set in the floor underneath or close to the trolley position.

In the case of constructing or converting halls specially for fencing, it is preferable to provide underfloor wiring housed in standard metal conduits. Although the voltage is only 12 volts, a 13 amp cable is advisable. The underfloor wiring should terminate to FIE regulation-size sockets located as shown in **5**.

When underfloor wiring cannot be provided, ground leads are used to connect the apparatus with the two spools.

Lighting
There should be an even lighting over the whole of the fencing floor space. This is usually provided by overhead fittings which should be at least 4m above the floor to prevent accidental damage.

Windows should be avoided or sited so that shafts of sunlight or glare cannot impose themselves upon the competitors during any time of the day. Failing that, provision should be made to curtain across windows.

Storage
Rolled-up rubber and metallic piste, scoring equipment and personal equipment will need storage space.

Spectators
This activity currently attracts crowds of between 60 and 200 to the majority of its major events, but crowds of up to 1000 have been known and therefore the activity is potentially one which could use an indoor arena.

Critical considerations
Quiet situation and noise control/lighting/flooring/type of piste installation/safety factors.

Sources of reference and further advice
The Amateur Fencing Association
Leon Paul Ltd (specialist equipment)

9
Five-a-side football

Siting

This game can be played anywhere in a common sports space having a maximum area of 36m × 28m. There should be no free space around the pitch as a feature of the game is the use of the walls as rebound surfaces. In a shared area, or where the end or side lines are not wall surfaces, a free-standing or socketed rebound barrier 1·22m minimum high must be provided. Equipment specialists supply standard panels and fixings and should be consulted for detailed advice. Goals may be set against end walls and protrude into the pitch, but extremities of the semi-circle should reach the back wall as shown in **2** and **3**.

Court markings

The Football Association's guide rules do not specify a colour. 50mm wide red lines have been advocated by The Sports Council to match netball due to the similarity between the two courts which suggested, for casual play, that the same markings could be used for both.

However, for increasingly popular competitions, and with rebound play, the similarities are not quite so marked. In a multi-sports area purpose-laid white lines can be better than masking-out most of the unwanted red lines, and ensure radius to the FA recommended dimensions. For comparison with netball, see p 38.

Spectator facilities

While 5-a-side football is an important participant sport, in many sports centres the game has not developed as a spectator event except in a limited way (eg the London 5-a-side competition). It is understood, however, that the indoor game, in a slightly changed form, is very popular in Europe and particularly in Holland. At major events a potential capacity of 5000 is estimated.

Best viewing is from a gallery all round, but if spectator accommodation is to be at floor level, mobile seating should be provided, elevated and set back from the pitch at the sides, so that spectators in the front rows can see over the portable 'walls'. Safety netting is an added precaution.

Floor

Non-slip. Decide extent and type of rebound barrier units, **2**, **3**, and check setting out of sockets against layout of other markings. Characteristics of rolling resistance and rebound resilience are important refer to Volume 2, Technical Study **17**.

Surrounding rebound surfaces or enclosure

Walls should be non-abrasive and contain no windows. If walls are used as boundaries of the playing area, there should be no projections or indentations *whatsoever*. Provide completely flush smooth rebound walls or portable enclosure units to a minimum height of 1·22m (preferably 'head height' ie 2·0m) as illustrated in **2–4**, and in Volume 2, p 152.

Background should be uniform in colour and provide a contrast to the ball. Design of blockwork walls, particularly

1 *A kick-about in Rochford Sports Hall. Photo: Chris Harper*

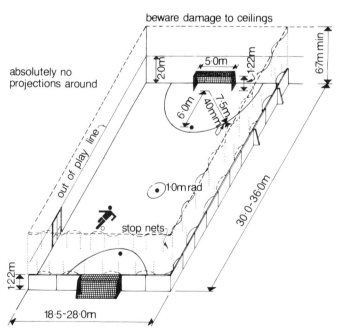

2 *Diagram of the FA's recommended dimensions and enclosing surfaces. The goal unit at one end is shown placed behind the goal line with rebound panels along the line abutting the goal posts,* **3**. *Alternatively, the other goal is shown protruding onto the playing area against a blank wall. In that situation rules require the goal semi-circle to be measured from the goal line between the posts, and the semi-circle line to be continued at 90° to the rebound back wall. See also Volume 2, Technical Study 18, including illustrated details of flush protected fire exit doorways, and proprietary rebound enclosure units and space dividers*

3 *Where the pitch does not abut a hall wall, the goal line is continuous with the goal unit set flush between the enclosing rebound units. Photo: Powersport International Limited*

behind goalmouths, should allow for considerable impact which has been known to dislodge blocks. Wall surfaces should be smooth and sealed to resist abrasion which causes grit to damage the flooring. Rebound dados of the floor material have also been tried. All doorways must be flush set. For Fire Exit door details see Volume 2, Technical Study **18**. For store openings see Volume 2, Part II, Technical Study **4** and **18**.

Internal environment
● Background heating for players should be 10–12·8°C, but where the game is played before spectators a higher level should be considered (at least 15°C).
● Natural or mechanical ventilation are equally suitable.
● Good all round lighting is essential. Artificial lighting should provide illuminance in the 300–700 lux range at floor level. It should be noted that hanging lights are not suitable.
● As regards noise control the game should not be played near quieter sports such as badminton, as it tends to be noisy, especially if rebound surfaces are used. Wall and ceiling surfaces should be designed to reduce reverberation.

Storage
Storage will be required for portable goals when not in use. Allow approximately 4·8m × 1·2m × 0·85m for each goal, and 2·5m × 1·25m for barrier panels stacked on trolleys

Critical considerations
Noise control/flush surroundings surfaces to avoid injuries from projections/ceiling panels well clipped in and not loose-laid.

Sources of reference
The Football Association's Recommended Rules of the Game.
Sports Council Research Working Papers 12 SC 1979, *Indoor Soccer at Three Sports Centres.*
Equipment trade.

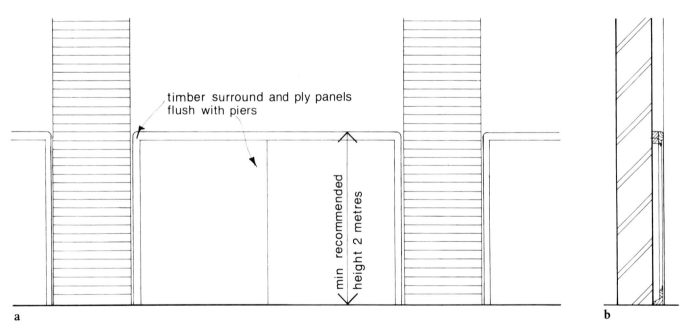

timber surround and ply panels flush with piers

min recommended height 2 metres

a   b

4a, b *In the conversion of buildings for sport, protruding piers are a very serious hazard and a permanent rebound surface must be provided set flush with existing walls. Details of*

Harben Armoury conversion, London Borough of Camden. (Architect: Martin Richmond)

10
Gymnastics

Siting

Area of activity	Standards of activity			
	⚭⚭	N	C	R
Length	73·0m	47·50–36·5m	32·0–36·5m*	do
Width	33·5m	23·0m	26·0m*	do
Overall (including surrounds)		min. 50·0 × 25·0m		
Height		7·6m	7·6m†	do†

* To fit medium and large sports halls (see Table II, Volume 2, pp 46–7)
† The Federation Internationale Gymnastique (FIG) clear height for training areas equipped with suspended safety belts is 6·5m (see 17)

Special requirements: floor and equipment
For all floor work the official measurements of the competition mat area are 12m × 12m × 54mm within a 14m × 14m area if on a raised podium. Additional pieces of apparatus require areas of approximately 36m² each and a minimum of 25m is required for vault run-up.
For specialist training pit dimensions see Data Sheet **34** on p 73. Such pits should be confined to a training gymnasium, or to a bay off a sports hall to share run-up space. There are difficulties in siting covered pits within a multi-sports floor area.
Men gymnasts compete on the vaulting horse, pommel horse, horizontal bars, parallel bars, rings, and floor. Women compete on the vaulting horse, beam, asymmetrical bars, and floor. Competitors perform compulsory and optional movements on each apparatus. There are separate titles for the team competition, individual combined events competition, and the individual events competitions.
Landing mats are now required with each apparatus shown in **5–13**.
Organisers of FIG Competitions, or similar competitions, must provide the double flex floor with the following measurements and characteristics.
● The floor is 12 × 12m consisting of sixty single tiles or mats each 2 × 1·2m, or forty-eight size 2 × 1·5m, or sixty-eight 1·5 × 1·5m, all 50–75mm maximum thickness, joined together with lugs, **5**.
● If this floor is intended to be on an elevated podium, the area it is placed in must measure 14 × 14m.
● The actual floor area must be clearly marked.
Note also floor anchor locations.

Storage
Storage is required for all or most of the items shown in **5–15**. For details a specialist gymnastics equipment supplier should be consulted.
Storage will also be needed for:
● The safety control weights and test equipment
● Landing mats 2 × 1·25m (perhaps a minimum of 20) each 65mm thick
● The double flex floor see **5**
● Modern rhythmic gymnastic apparatus such as rope/ball/ribbon and cane/club/hoop
● Safety belts (if not left suspended) as shown in **17**.
● Officials Tables etc as shown in **2**

1 *Photo: Sports Council Publications*

● Pommel covers
● Trampolines used for gymnastics training

Spectators
As a spectator and participant sport, gymnastics has experienced a boom in recent years and a number of sponsored events have developed as well as international events. This activity could be one which would benefit greatly from an increased spectator capacity available at a major indoor arena with a potential capacity of 10 000 plus.

Other considerations
● Check required environmental standards with the British Amateur Gymnastics Association (BAGA) particularly for coaching and International events
● Roof loadings and headrooms for training apparatus and trampolines

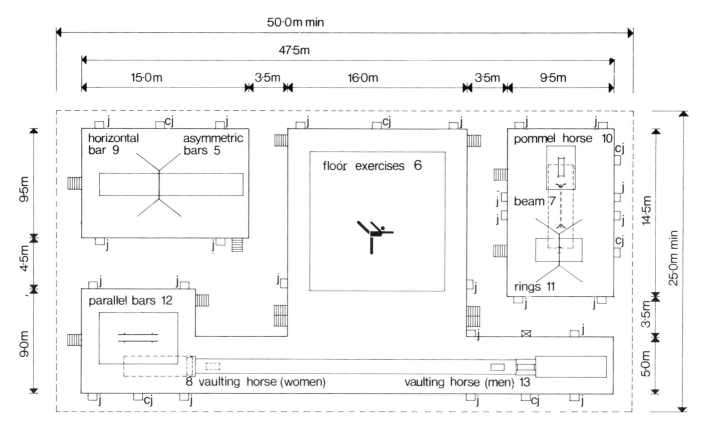

horizontal bar 9   asymmetric bars 5

floor exercises 6

pommel horse 10

beam 7

rings 11

parallel bars 12

8 vaulting horse (women)   vaulting horse (men) 13

50·0m min

47·5m

15·0m   3·5m   16·0m   3·5m   9·5m

9·5m   4·5m   9·0m

14·5m   3·5m   5·0m   25·0m min

j judge   cj chief judge

2 *Diagram of women's and men's combined competition podium. This specialist gymnastics equipment is not to be confused with the quite different school gymnasium equipment*

equipment numbers refer to following diagrams

Key

Women's competitive area:
5 Asymmetric bars (or uneven bars)
6 Mat area for ground work
7 Beam (or balance beam)
8 Vaulting horse

Men's competitive area:
6 Mat area for ground work
9 Horizontal Bar (or High Bar)
10 Pommel horse
11 Rings
12 Parallel bars
13 Vaulting horse

3 *General view of gymnastics training in a sports hall. Photo: Colin Westwood*

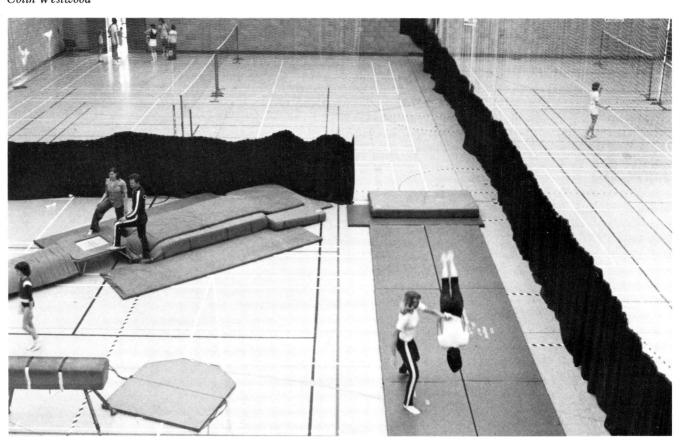

4 *Training on the asymmetric bars guyed to floor ring bolts. Note the chalk dish. Photo: David Butler*

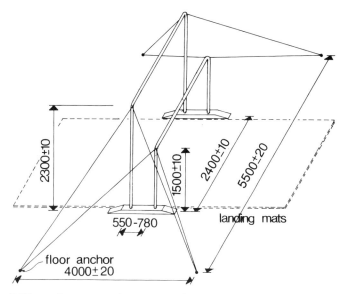

7 *Women's asymmetric or uneven bars*

floor anchor
4000±20

2300±10
1500±10
2400±10
5500±20
550–780
landing mats

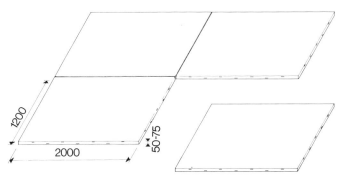

5 *Double flex floor area for groundwork. Since the 1979 World Championships, floor areas are under review by the FIG Technical Committee. In Fort Worth the AMF spring floor was used*

1200
2000
50–75

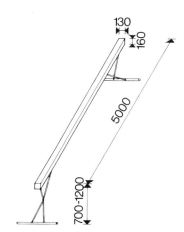

6 *Women's balance beam*

130
160
5000
700–1200

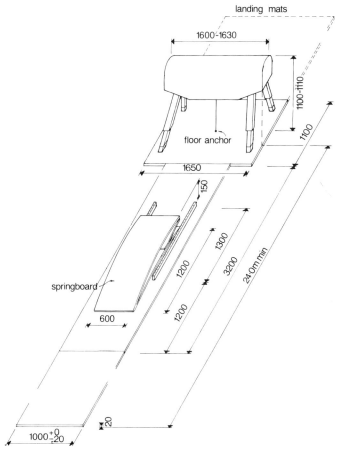

8 *Women's vaulting horse with runway and springboard. A device must be present to attach the springboard, which must be adjustable in 50mm intervals. The attachment is connected to a plywood board which is covered with the same material as the adjoining runway. (As a height balance between the side and diagonal horse, a covered plywood plate of 1·1 × 1·65m is used). A measuring tape must be available from the starting point of the horse, so that the gymnast can orientate himself*

landing mats
1600–1630
1100±10
1100
floor anchor
1650
150
springboard
600
1200
1300
3200
1200
24·0m min
1000 +0 −20
20

Sources of reference
British Amateur Gymnastics Association (BAGA)
International Gymnastics Federation (FIG) *Measurements, dimensions and forms* (extracts 1974 edition).
Note: Apparatus specifications are under review (Feb 1980).
United States Gymnastics Federation Safety Manual, obtainable from BAGA.
TUS Data Sheet 24, *Gymnastics training facilities at Lilleshall Hall NSC*; and studies concerning (covered) pits related to multi-purpose sports halls.

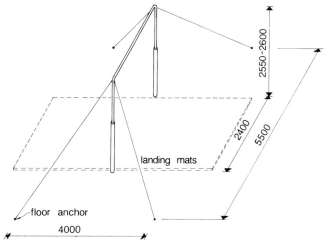

9 *Men's horizontal bar*

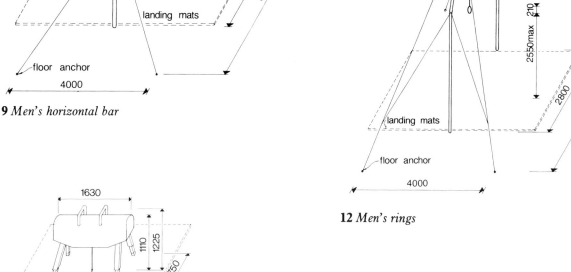

12 *Men's rings*

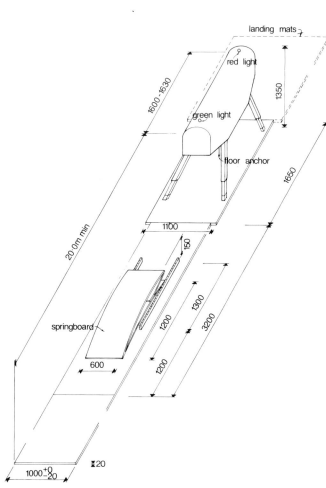

10 *Men's pommel horse*

11 *Men's vaulting horse. The springboard attachment is similar to the women's runway,* **8**

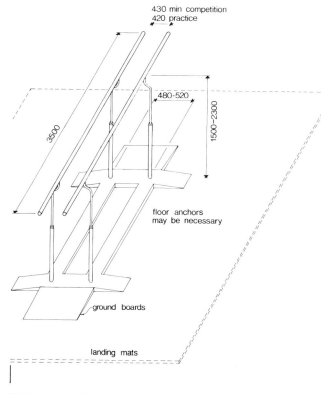

13 *Men's parallel bars*

14 *Six scoreboards are connected to the green and red light*

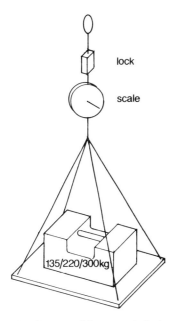

135/220/300kg

15 *Test spring scales for use with women's balance beam, men's horizontal and parallel bars and the rings*

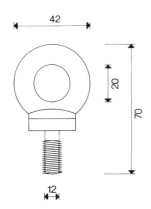

42

20

70

12

16 *Detail of floor ring bolt required to anchor guy wires from all equipment except the balance beam (and floor mats)*

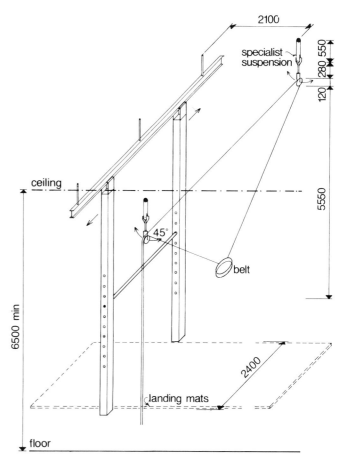

2100

specialist suspension

550
280
120

ceiling

45°

belt

5550

6500 min

2400

landing mats

floor

17 *Roof fixing location for training and safety equipment with ropes and safety belt, to learn difficult and risky link movements. See also page 74 for training pit details (in special training gymnasia)*

18 *Use of foam landing crash mattress as a safety landing area. Photo: Kay-Metzeler Limited*

11
Handball: seven-a-side and mini-handball

Siting

The International Handball Federation has standardised court sizes to 40 × 20m, but this reduction is still longer than almost all UK sports halls. The dimensions given below for county, club and recreational levels of play are less than that standard recommended by the British Handball Association for all levels of play, but are the agreed minimum court dimensions to promote seven-a-side handball in the sizes of hall given in Table II on pp 46–7 in Volume 2.

A five-a-side version of the game has been discontinued by the BHA, although in small halls, where the width is a serious restriction, for recreational play team numbers are adjusted to the size of court available.

Mini-handball has been developed for 5–10-year-olds and details are given on p 29.

Space

Playing area Seven-a-side	Standards of play			
	⬡⬡	N	C	R
Length	40m	40–34·5m*	40–30·0m min	30·0m min
Width	20m	20·0m	20·0m	17·0m min
Side margins, min**	2m	1·0m	1·0m	none^w
End margins; min	1m	1·0m	1·0m	1·0m
Overall area	42 × 24m	min 36·5*–42m × 23m	min 32–42m × 22m**	min 32 × 17m^w
Height^h	12·5m	min 9·0m	9–7·6m	7·6–6·7^h

* 'Friendly' national matches only. All major tournaments, European international, World Cup and pre-Olympic matches must be played on 40·0m long courts.
** Increase to 2m one side for match table and team bench space.
^w Side wall–wall play in halls of 20·0m or less width.
^h Maximum height is an important factor: a goal-keeper can attempt whole length lobs to score directly into the opponents goal. Minimum height recommended by BHA is 7·6m

Floor

A slip-resistant, resilient floor is preferred. Asphalt or tarmacadam surfaces are unsatisfactory (BHA). 'Rolling resistance' is important; see Volume 2, Technical Study **17**.

Court markings

Lines 50mm wide are included in overall court sizes, **2**, and orange is the colour given in Table I on p 139 in Volume 2. However, the International colour yellow is required for all matches under IHF regulations. The BHA will accept yellow and black striped lines, using 'hazard' tapes as an alternative for club and national matches, but there is still likely to be confusion with the multitude of badminton lines in a multi-sports hall. Orange is acceptable for recreational play.

There is marked similarity with hockey dimensions and lines which the BHA feels might be rationalised further on the following basis.

If the handball 9m free-throw circle were marked by a *solid* line and the inner goal area circle with a *broken* line, then the latter could be masked out for hockey leaving the common 9m circle. Yellow is also the preferred common colour. Penalty markers and goal posts are already standardised, **1**.

1 *Goal units are interchangeable for indoor hockey. Photo: James Dunlop and BHA*

Walls

Walls should be absolutely flush (as for five-a-side soccer) and up to 3m high without any projections such as basketball winch gears. Basketball boards should be protected.

Spectators

Handball is a growth spectator sport in Europe, and it could increase in the UK given the presently programmed TV coverage. The BHA suggests allowing for 50–250 spectators at National League and club matches with up to 1000 or more at finals and internationals. Spectators should be sited at least 2m from the side lines and restricted from near or behind goals.

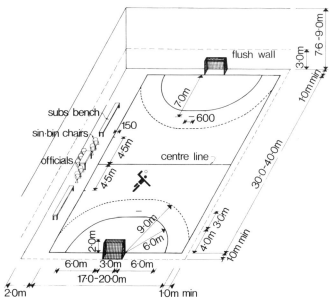

2 *Diagram of handball space. Note that the international maximum area of court has been reduced to 40 × 20m*

Internal environment

● Temperature requirements are the same as for basketball due to substitutes and 'sin-bin' sitters-out.

● Lighting should be even, without glare or reflected glare.

Storage

Storage will be required for dual-purpose handball/hockey goal-posts and net units; an officials' table, seven chairs and team benches; match control equipment/scoreboard.

Critical considerations

IHF colour markings/projection-free walls/temperature/ maximum ceiling height to avoid damage by high lobs.

Sources of reference

BHA and Sports Council wall chart, *Play Handball.*

Mini-handball (seven-a-side)

Siting

This version of the game can take place in a common sports hall or school gymnasium (if protection can be given to young players from the projections of wall bars and other equipment), indoors or on the playground. It will fit into Sports Council low-cost halls for small and local community provision, **3, 4.**

Court markings

The game might share with four- or five-a-side soccer in small halls if it is played side-wall to wall. Otherwise allow 1m minimum margin all around and 50mm wide orange lines.

Walls

These should be flush and without projections to a minimum height of 2m. Avoid, or steel-mesh protect, clerestory or other windows.

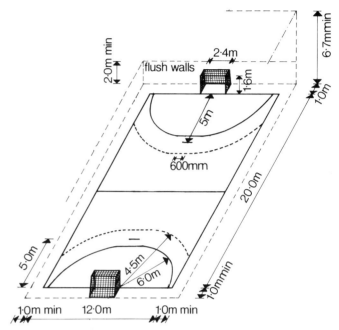

4 *Diagram of court. The goal size is 2·4m wide × 1·6m high × 1m deep*

Internal environment

Lighting should be even, and suspended fittings avoided.

Storage

Storage will be required for goal units only.

Critical considerations

Flush walls/adequate clear unobstructed height/protect other equipment, windows etc/pad projections against injury to players.

Source of reference and further advice

British Handball Association and Sports Council wall chart, *Play Handball.*

3 *A sport ideal for 5–10 year old boys, girls or mixed teams, indoors or on the playground. Junior handball for 10–14 years olds is now played on a minimum full sized handball court, but with a junior ball. Photo: British Handball Association at Milton Keynes Leisure Centre*

12
Hockey indoors:
six-a-side

Siting
For top standards of play this sport requires a space longer than the recommended size for a large sports hall*.

Space

Playing area	Standards of play		
	N	C	R
Length including end lines	36·0–44·0m	33·5*–44·0m	2:1 length/ width ratio
Width *excluding* 100mm sideboards	18·0–22·0m	16·75–22·0m	
Runout behind goal lines	3·0m	min 1·5m	1·5m
Clearance outside sideboards**	min 1·5m	min 1·5m	1·5m
Overall area	42–50 × 22·4–26·4m	*36·5–47 × 21·15–26·4m	***
Height	7·6m	7·6m	6·7m

* To fit a hall of 36·5m length allowing for end overruns, but shorter than The Hockey Association's recommended minimum 36 × 18m (overall 39 × 21m) wherever possible. Sponsors of large sports hall projects should consult with the Sports Council and Hockey Associations to take into account the possible need for an increased size of hall to give N and C standards of training and play.
** 1·2m wider one side for match officials tabel and team bench spaces.
*** Team numbers can be adjusted according to the size of pitch available.

Floor
Flooring should be firm, level, slip-resistant and dark in colour. The surface needs to be absolutely flush including all inset sockets, and smooth without a pronounced surface texture for the ball to run true. Characteristics of ball to surface resilience and rolling resistance are also important: refer to Volume 2, Part II, Technical Study **17**. See also side line boards detail **3**, which for top class play require fastening to the floor. In the sports workshop advanced indoor training hall at Bisham Abbey NSC hockey is played on the artificial grass carpet.

Court markings
Lines are 50mm wide and are coloured white for N and C, and light blue or orange for R. Yellow is sometimes used for TV presentations, but care must be taken to avoid confusion with recreational badminton lines. Between goal posts, the goal line may be up to 80mm wide. For major competitions all lines used for other sports should be removed. In Scotland, green markings have been found suitable.

Walls
●Enclosing barriers: where the pitch is part of a large hall floor, the pitch and free zone should preferably be enclosed within portable 'walls' or a barrier 1·2m high. Equipment manufacturers supply standard panels usable for five-a-side soccer, roller skating, and hockey enclosures.

1 *Photo: Wood/Mayfair London*

2 *Space diagram. The table of dimensions includes reduced sizes of indoor pitch, to fit Sports Council hall sizes, as relaxed by The Hockey Association in the preparation of this Data Sheet*
3 *Detail of side-boards. See The Hockey Association's preferred specification for fastening these to the floor*

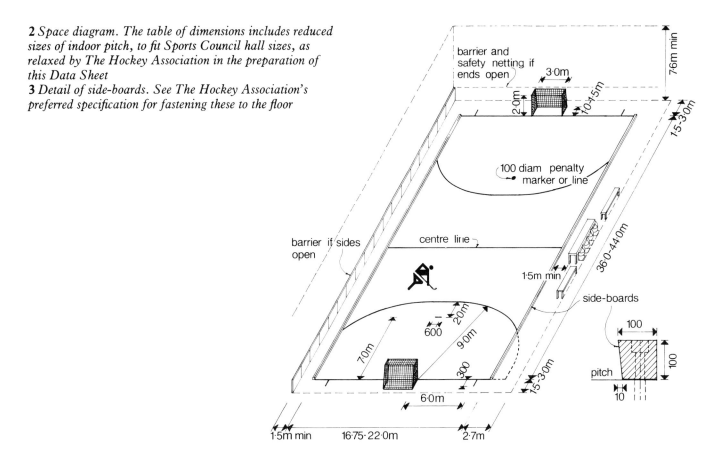

- If the pitch is walled off at the ends, suitable padding, e.g. judo matting, should be placed against the wall both sides of the goal to prevent injuries and rebounds.
- Side-line boards: the side boards, **2–4**, should be joined together down each side of the pitch in such a way as to present a continuous surface to the pitch, although it is accepted that there will be joints between the sections which form the side board itself. Ideally side boards should be fastened to the floor by means of recessed inverted bolts which are engaged in sockets in the floor. Failing this, some means of securing the side boards from lateral movement should be used, eg floor mats wedged against a firm restraining edge or wall.

Spectator facilities
Indoor hockey is increasing rapidly in popularity as a spectator sport and adequate provision for spectators should be made.

The sport has benefited enormously from the provision of major sports centres and now has a thriving programme of major indoor events. The large area required for the pitch means that spectator capacity is reduced at many venues. The potential capacity at major events is estimated at 2000 plus.

Best viewing is from an elevated position, ie a gallery, but bleacher seating all round is suitable providing some form of netting is hung between the spectators and the goal line when viewing from either end of the pitch. This netting should be a minimum of 3m behind the goal line and about of 5m in height to avoid danger to spectators and damage to other equipment.

Internal environment
- For players, background heating only is required (12·8°C) but where the game is to be played before spectators a higher level should be considered 15°C).
- Natural or mechanical ventilation are equally suitable.
- Natural lighting from the sides and above is suitable, or artificial lighting from above should give good overall light

without glare and should provide an intensity of 200–300 lux.
- As the game tends to be noisy, walls and ceiling surfaces should be designed to minimise reverberation.

Goal posts
Goal posts should be provided as mentioned on p 28. They should display red and white striped markings and have a dual use also for handball. Self-standing, folding and wheelaway units are available.

Sources of reference
Based on Indoor Hockey Rules 1979 issued by Federation Internationale De Hockey, Indoor Hockey Committee; Technical Specification No 1 of The Hockey Association and advice provided by the UK governing bodies of the sport.

4 *Side boards should be anchored to the floor rather than wedged loosely against improvised restrainers in the side margins. Photo: Wood/Mayfair, London*

13
Judo

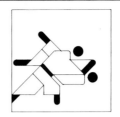

Siting

Practice and recreational judo can take place in practice halls (see Volume 2, Part II, Technical Study **5**, and in sports/arts workshops (see Volume 2, Part II, Technical Study **10**). In smaller sized rooms, the outer safety area is very restricted or cannot be provided. Walls must therefore be built absolutely flush and padded by inclined mats.

In sports halls where there is more space, **3**, judo mats can be located in the subdivided zones shown in **1–13** on pp. 48–9 in Volume 2. For fitting mats into awkward and irregular shapes in converted buildings, see 'Sources of Reference'.

Space

	Standard ⚬	N	C	R
Contest area	10 × 10m	9–10 × 9–10m	9–10 × 9–10m	9–10 × 9–10m
Minimum safety area around	2·5m	2·5m	2·5m	1·5–2·5m
One competition mat	16 × 16m	16 × 16m	14–16 × 14–16m	—
Two ,, ,,	29 × 16m	29 × 16m	27–29 × 14–16m	—
Three ,, ,,	42 × 16m	42 × 16m	39–42 × 14–16m	—
Officials and competitors space one side	+ 3–4m	+ 2·0m min.	+ 2·0m min.	—
Clearway on other side	+ 3–4m	+ 0·5m min.	+ 0·5m min.	—
Minimum overall				
One contest area	22 × 22m	17 × 18·5m	15–17 × 16·5–18·5m	12–15 × 12–15m
Clear headroom min	—	7·6m	4·5m	3·5m

Special factors for competitions

An area of approximately 16 × 16m per competition is required. Two or three competition areas may be needed, arranged side by side as shown in **2**. A 3m-wide safety area can be shared between two competition areas in an overall space, including officials and circulation, of at least 18·5 × 30m, or 18·5 × 43m for three mats, as shown in **3**.

Major competitions require between two and nine mats to be operating simultaneously and thus the large floor area required for these events would be well suited to an indoor arena. Public address and approved scoring and timekeeping equipment is required.

For international contests, two areas are usual; with three required for national championships and preliminary Olympic contests. Junior and schools' national one-day championships can need up to seven areas.

Spectators

The sport has a strong following and a recent history of success in international competition. The potential capacity required for major events is estimated at 4000.

Markings

There are no floor markings other than printed on the floor mats.

Floor mats

Sectional mats 2 × 1m are close laid to make up contest/competition areas. Modern mats interlock avoiding the earlier

1 *Photo: The Architectural Press*

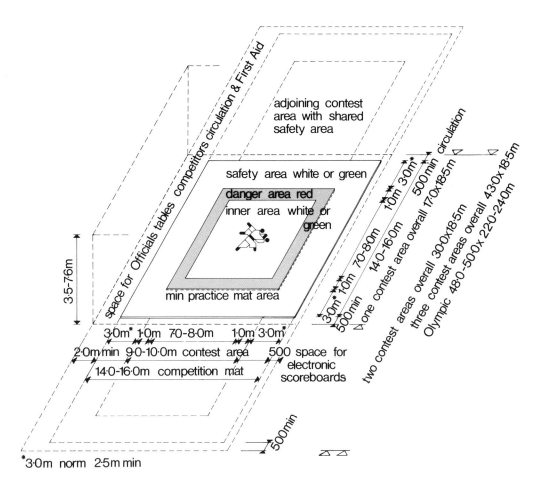

2 *Space diagram*   *3·0m norm 2·5m min

Within the diagram:
- competitors circulation & First Aid
- space for Officials tables
- adjoining contest area with shared safety area
- safety area white or green
- **danger area red**
- inner area white or green
- min practice mat area
- 3·5-7·6m
- 3·0m* 1·0m 7·0-8·0m 1·0m 3·0m*
- 2·0m min 9·0-10·0m contest area
- 14·0-16·0m competition mat
- 500 space for electronic scoreboards
- 30m* 1·0m 7·0-8·0m
- 500 min
- 14·0-16·0m
- 1·0m 3·0m*
- 500 min circulation
- one contest area overall 17·0x18·5m
- two contest areas overall 30·0x18·5m
- three contest areas overall 43·0x18·5m
- Olympic 48·0-50·0x 22·0-24·0m
- 500min

need for an outer timber-framed lock. Specialist suppliers should be also consulted. The International Judo Federation contest rules require that the competition area, **2**, must be mounted on a resilient platform, but does not specify a thickness nor height from the floor.

Internal environment
- Background heating of only 10–12·5°C
- Adequate ventilation is important to prevent the atmosphere becoming humid causing excessive perspiration. A damp mat surface soon becomes dangerous
- There is no special lighting requirement.

Storage
One 16 × 16m competition area requires 128 mats size 2 × 1m, and each additional contest area adds 104 mats, best stored on trolleys ready for easy use and to avoid mishandling. Storage is also required for match officials' table, scoreboard, timer and pool-sheet notice board. A wall-hung blackboard is used for recreational and training sessions.

Critical factors
The minimum safety area. In small rooms where this is unobtainable, walls must be temporarily padded. Walls must be flush with means to secure upright mats, or permanently fixed in a very small situation, to a height of 2m. Adequate ventilation, particularly in internal or basement rooms.

Source of references and further advice
British Judo Association (BJA)
Judo Indentikit series by BJA, particularly No. 8, giving ideas for improving The Dojo, including clubs with limited space or odd shaped areas in converted buildings. Mat layouts are shown.
BJA *Tournament Handbook* provides essential details of

3 *European Judo Championships in progress at Crystal Palace. Photo: British Judo Association*

facilities requirements, related to the number of entries, for the five ratings of tournament. It specifies for example the required number of mats, officials, spectator seating, parking and changing spaces, refreshment and other accommodation needs.

14
Karate

Karate is a practical, empty-handed fighting technique, a formal method of physical and mental training and a competitive combat sport. Karate contests are held as Kata, male and female, competitions (introduced in 1978) and as sparring matches, in which some karate techniques are not permitted and only a few used very often. To avoid injuries all punches, blows, strikes and kicks are controlled and pulled back before contact.

Space

Combat area	Standards of play		
	N	C	R
Length	10·0m	10·0m	6·0m
Width	10·0m	10·0m	6·0m
Overall area	15 × 15m	15 × 13m	9 × 9m

Siting
A minimum area of 1·5m free space around the combat area must be provided. For international contests an area of 15m × 15m is required. Three combat areas of international size are required for regional competitions amounting to an overall area of 40 × 15m, including an overlapping 2·5m wide safety zone between parallel combat areas, **2**.

Floor
Sprung wood or firm matting which does not move apart.

Other requirements
These are the same as for aikido and judo.

Sources of reference
English Karate Federation
Martial Arts Commission

1 *Photo: East Anglian Daily Times and Associated Papers*

2 *Space diagram*

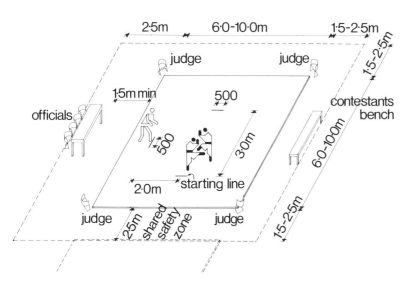

15
Kendo

This is one of the traditional Japanese martial arts, and is presented as a modern competitive sport. Two contestants, wearing protective armour, fight with bamboo swords. Footwork is vital—kendoka use short, fast gliding steps, and sometimes a jump for counter attacks.

Siting
The sport can take place in a common sports hall or large projectile hall, where approximately 13m width and a minimum height of 4·5m is provided, **12**. Coaching and training in smaller practice halls is possible with reduced safety zones.

Floor and markings
A smooth, wooden-floored rectangular area, usually 9 × 11m to 11 × 11m is required. The centre is marked with a cross and the boundary with lines 50–100mm wide. Two starting lines are also marked.

Source of reference
Martial Arts Commission

1 *Photo: Faulkner-Brown Hendy Watkinson Stonor*

2 *Space diagram*

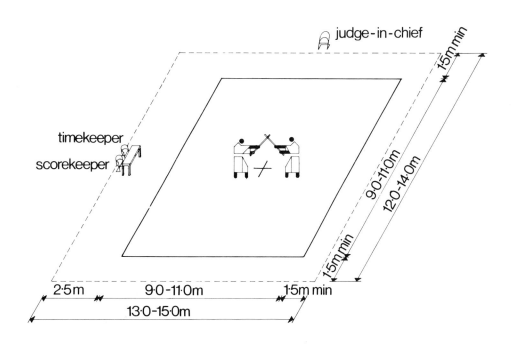

judge-in-chief

timekeeper
scorekeeper

15m min

9·0-11·0m

12·0-14·0m

1·5m min

2·5m   9·0-11·0m   1·5m min

13·0-15·0m

16
Korfball: indoor micro korfball

Korfball originated in Holland where it shares equal popularity with football. It is played by teams composed of an equal number of men and women. The indoor version is played on a much smaller pitch than the outdoor and is known in this country as indoor (micro) korfball. It is a mixed sex team game with rules similar to netball but with techniques from basketball and handball. Further details can be obtained from the British Korfball Association.

Siting
Micro korfball can be played in a medium or large sports hall or multi-purpose sports space, **2**. It is comparable in area and similar in markings with five-a-side football, handball and hockey (without goal areas) and lacrosse.

Floor
Flooring should be durable, resilient and non-slip.

Court markings
Court markings consist of orange or light-blue tape on the floor. *White markings are preferred for competition play.*

Spectator facilities
The game is best viewed from galleries overlooking the pitch along both sides, but retractable seating along the sides (and even at the ends) is suitable.

Surrounding surfaces or enclosures
Micro-korfball does not need to be enclosed but if it is, there should be a space 2m wide all round the court.

Internal environment
• Players require background heating only (10–13°C), but if possible, spectators should have a higher level (at least 15°C).
• Mechanical ventilation is preferable, providing 1½ air changes an hour.
• Natural top light is suitable and artificial light should be from fittings suspended above, but preferably beyond, the perimeter of the pitch.

Storage
A space approximately 3·5 × 0·5 × 0·5m is required to store two goals.

Special requirements
As this game is played by *mixed teams* adequate changing and lavatory facilities are always required for both sexes.

Critical considerations
Safety of players as for five-a-side football.
Pitch length must be twice the width.

Source of reference
British Korfball Association

1 *From Holland comes a fast, skilful mixed teams sport—korfball. Played by teams of men and women (or boys and girls), with rules designed for complete equality. Photo: British Korfball Association*

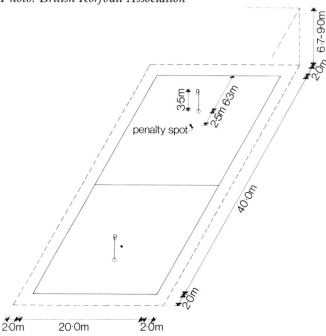

2 *Space diagram of korfball played with two divisions indoors. Each team consists of 4 boys and 4 girls—2 boys and 2 girls from each team in each division. After two goals the divisions or roles change round. It may be permissible to play on slightly smaller pitches but the length must always be twice the width*

17
Lacrosse: women's seven-a-side

Siting
Indoor lacrosse can be played in halls of 32m length with a small reduction to the minimum court size recommended by the All England Women's Lacrosse Association. Reduced standards for recreational play in shorter halls are given below. The recommended dimensions also apply to Lacrosse outdoors on restricted pitches and kick-about areas, 2.

It should be noted that there is no longer a men's indoor game, but box lacrosse might soon be introduced from the United States. Further information about this development can be obtained from the English Lacrosse Union.

Space

1 *The Lacrosse net ring is 610mm diameter and set at 45°. Photo: All England Women's Lacrosse Association*

	Standards of play			
	N	C	R	Practice
Playing area**	33–36 × 15–21m	min 32* × 15–21m	29 × 15–21m	22·5–26 × 16·5m
Goals inset	1·5–3·0m	1·5–3·0m	min 1·0m	min 1·0m
Distance between goals	30m	min 29m*	27m	min 20·5m
Clear height	9·0m	7·6–9m	min 6·7m	min 6·7m

* To fit halls of 32m length but short of the 33m minimum length currently specified in the Rules of Indoor Lacrosse.
** Playing the ball off the walls is permitted where possible. Where the playing area will not extend across the complete width of some halls, a fine mesh sports net or curtain may be required to safely enclose the pitch. The playing area might be widened in halls of 23m widths to play off four walls.

Floor and markings
Flooring should be slip resistant. Markings are white lines 50mm wide or an approved colour to contrast with existing coloured markings in multi-sports halls.

Spectators
This sport should preferably be viewed from a gallery. At pitch level safety netting should be considered for the safety of spectators.

Walls
The rules of the game allow rebound play off the walls which should be flush and blank with as few projections (such as basket ball rings etc) as possible. Glazing below a height of 6m must be toughened.

Environment
● Recessed light fittings are preferred at high level to avoid damage.
● A moderate temperature of 12·5°C is adequate. All fittings must be a high level or flush mounted into walls below a height of 6m.
● Good ventilation is essential.

Equipment storage
Storage will be required for posts (which could double with netball) rings, balls and possibly a few sticks, but most players have their own.

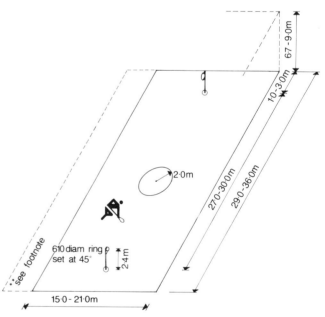

2 *Space diagram. See also the table of dimensions for standards of play in small halls including reduced sizes of pitch to fit Sports Council hall sizes*

Changing area
Changing accommodation adequate for 24 players will be required. If possible, two rooms should be provided so that match players and teams can discuss tactics in privacy.

Critical considerations
Availability of phone and first-aid/public address equipment for commentary/wall and floor surfaces/availability of the indoor ball/adequate ventilation.

Sources of reference
Books and publications approved by the AEWLA

18
Netball

Siting
Provided there is free space all round the court this game can be played anywhere in a common sports space.

Space

Playing area	Standards of play		
	N	C	R
Length	30·50m	30·5m	30·5m
Width	15·25m	15·25m	15·25m
Space at side lines	1·5–2m*	min 1·2m	min 0·75m
Space behind goal lines	1·5–2m	min 1·2**	min 0·75m
Overall area min	33·5 × 18·25m*	32·9 × 17·65**	min 32 × 16·75m
Height min	7·6m	7·0–7·6m	min 6·7m†

* Wider if possible where match tables and team benches have to be accommodated on one side. Also, if equipment is to be wall mounted, eg in a school gymnasium, then safety margin widths must be clear of all projections
** Minimum 1·5 where, spectators are also situated at ends
† 6·1m in Scotland

Court markings
These are 50mm wide coloured red for recreational play and white for tournament centre courts. For details see Volume 2, Part II, Technical Study **17**. See also the court markings described in five-a-side football on p 21.

Goal posts
The goal post may be supported by a metal base which should not project on to the court and which should be stable without need for hazardous weights.

Spectator facilities
Accommodation for spectators will be required for N and C standards of play. All-round seating may be unavoidable, but this game is best viewed from the sides (see Table footnote **).

Flooring
It should be noted that IFNA Rule 1 requires that the court shall have a firm surface. It should also be slip-resistant and preferably resilient.

Surrounding surfaces or enclosure
Walls should be non-abrasive, without windows and light in colour to contrast with the ball.

Internal environment
● For players background heating only is required (13°C) but where the game is played before spectators, a higher level should be considered.
● Mechanical or natural ventilation is equally suitable.
● Good all-round, even lighting is required. Artificial lighting should give an intensity of 200–300 lux. Hanging lights are not suitable and fittings must be protected and resistant to impact.
● No special requirements are necessary for noise control, but walls and ceilings should be designed to reduce reverberation time.

1 *Photo: Brian Worrell*

2 *Space diagram. Note: to fit small hall sizes, the space around the court for recreational play may now be reduced to 0·75m minimum, as agreed by the UK governing bodies of sport in the preparation of this data sheet. In Scotland 0·9m minimum is preferred*

Storage
The portable goals used in this game are readily and easily storable. Some types can be wheeled and stacked.

Critical considerations
Adequate height/avoid locating posts within the court.

Source of reference
International Federation of Netball Associations (IFNA) and the UK governing bodies of Netball.

19
Table tennis

The English Table Tennis Association specifies four standards of competition play in the context of the facilities needed:
P/C   Practice and inter-club matches
L/C   Inter-league and inter-county matches
N   International matches
T   Tournaments

Siting
Dimensions for the total playing space around each table for these various standards and for recreational play are as follows:

Overall space	Standards of play N*	L/C*	P/C	R
Length	12–14·0m	14·0–11·0m min	10·0m	7·6m
Width	6–7·0m	7·0–5·50m min	5·0m	4·6m
Ceiling height	4·20m	4·2m	4·2m	—
Clear below lights	4·05m	4·05m	4·05m	2·7m

* One table only required. For UK national championships a minimum area of 12 × 6m is acceptable
A table top is 2·743 (9ft) × 1·524 (5ft) × 0·762 (2ft 6in) from the floor

Basic needs
Certain requirements are common to all competitions and match play:

Flooring
Flooring should be preferably slightly resilient and not entirely non-slip. A level floor is, of course, essential.

Walls
Walls should provide a uniformly dark, non-glossy background. Dark-green screens and drapes have been used to give the necessary contrast to help players follow the ball.

Environment
Lighting varies for the different standards of play. Service illuminance at table height should be 150–500 lux. Fluorescent tubes, unless 3-phase, are unsatisfactory due to stroboscopic effect of the table tennis ball, and tungsten halogen lamps are preferable. Daylight should be excluded.

Where a mounting height greater than 5m above the floor is available, high-bay reflectors with incandescent or discharge lamps, or spotlights, can be used provided that precautions are taken. The luminaire light distribution should not be too narrow otherwise the overlap of light will be too small for acceptably uniform illuminance on and above the table and illuminance on vertical planes will probably be inadequate. On the other hand, if the light distribution is too wide the installation may be glaring. Angled spotlights should be trained across the table and not along it to prevent players being troubled by direct and reflected glare.

See also *IES Lighting Guide: Sport*.
● A temperature of 13°C is desirable in the playing area.
● Strong air currents should be avoided.

1 *Photo: Architectural Press*

Changing
For each sex there should be toilets and changing rooms with showers.

Storage
Sectional tables are stored upright or on trolleys, but readily mobile and fold-down types, **3**, allow swift setting-up and storage in less floor space than on trolleys. The playing surface is also better protected. Barrier panels stack on trolleys in $2·0 \times 0·76$m spaces.

Coaching and practice
Some types of table can also be used for rebound practice by simply lifting one side into a right-angle position.

Officials' furniture
Tables and chairs will be required for match and tournament officials. The referee's chair should be fitted with a writing rest.

Tournaments
Table tennis tournaments vary considerably in size, but it is rare that more than 12 tables are required, **4**. An unobstructed space of 36×30m will accommodate this number of tables. Intercourt barriers are required. A minimum of 2m must be left between the barriers and the hall wall to allow movement of players, officials and spectators. Ideally, tables can be arranged in a U shaped layout, or a central corridor should be allowed for direct access to all tables. Lighting of tables for knock-out rounds of competitions may be by permanent hall lighting system. For the semi-finals and finals special area lighting for one or two tables is necessary, with permanent lighting dimmable.
Movable bleacher seating for 500 spectators should be available.

Officials' space
A number of officials are required to operate a tournament and a working area is necessary in the hall. Ideally, this should be raised to give a good view of all tables.
The working area must be at least 9m² and work tables with a minimum length of 4m are necessary. A public address system, operable from the work area, is also necessary. Ideally, another microphone near the table used for the finals should be available.
If it is not possible to accommodate officials in the main hall, a room or gallery, preferably with a view of the hall, will be necessary. The room must have easy access to the hall. All requirements previously stated in this Data Sheet should prevail.
Scoreboards to carry continuously updated result sheets for the public are necessary. They should be positioned just inside or at the entrance to the hall.

Practice and inter-club matches: P/C
Most table tennis clubs run two or more teams. The minimum unobstructed playing spaces required for more than one table placed side by side, are as follows:

Two tables	10×10m
Three tables	10×15m
Four tables	10×20m
or	
	20×10m (pairs end to end)

Inter-court barriers should be provided if possible.
Special lighting to suit the layout of the tables is recommended as overall lighting is not particularly satisfactory for the players. An illuminance of 400 lux is now required.
Spectator seating unnecessary for this type of event. Tables

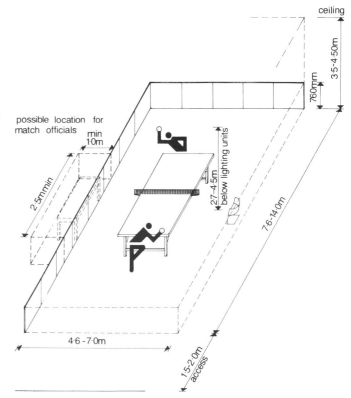

2 *Space diagram*

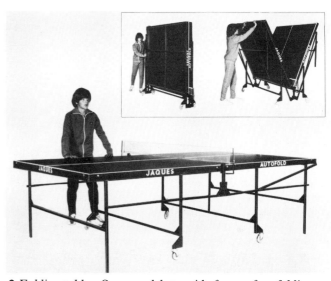

3 *Folding tables. Some models provide face-to-face folding which protects the surface during storage, wheels for easy manipulation and ready-fitted net and posts which remain in position when the table is folded away. Photo: John Jaques & Son Limited*

4 *A typical multi-table tournament scene. Photo: Sports Council Publications*

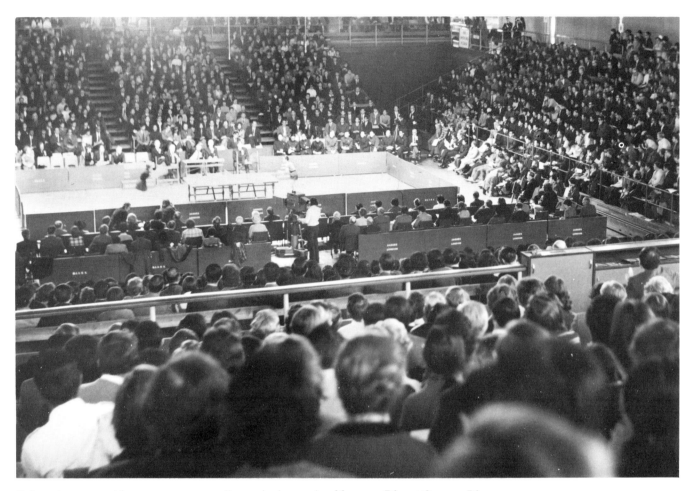

5 *A major event with spectators surrounding a single match table area. Photo: Century Photos*

should be arranged in one direction and preferably not end-to-end, unless staggered.

Inter-league and inter-county matches: L/C

Only one table is needed for this type of event and the playing area should ideally conform to the international standard dimensions of 14 × 7m.

Enclosing barriers are required and special lighting at 400 lux is most desirable. It should be noted that permanent hall lighting should be dimmable down to 150 lux.

Spectator seating should be provided for 100 at ground level around the playing arena and the provision of simple refreshments for players and spectators is necessary.

International matches: N

Only one table is required for this type of event and the playing area must be 14 × 7m. Enclosing barriers are required and special arena lighting is essential to give 500 lux. Permanent hall lighting must be dimmable down to 150 lux. Tiered spectator seating should be provided for 500–3000 people, **5**.

Sources of reference

This sports Data Sheet has been compiled from information supplied by the English Table Tennis Association and further advice can be obtained from them.

20
Tchouk-ball

Tchouk-ball is a non-contact indoor or outdoor team game devised and developed in the 1960s by Dr Herman Brandt, an eminent Swiss biologist. The British Tchouk-ball Association (BT–BA) was formed in 1972. The game combines elements of handball with Basque pelota: the wall being replaced by a framed sprung net, **1**, against which the ball is thrown to rebound in various trajectories. A point is scored when the ball is rebounded to fall into unoccupied court, where the opposing team is unable to prevent it from touching the floor.

Siting
The dimensions of the playing area can be varied to suit the space and number of players available. A high-density use is made of a limited space. There are two versions of the game: two-way tchouk-ball, **2**, and a one-way recreational game, **3**, which needs only half the space.

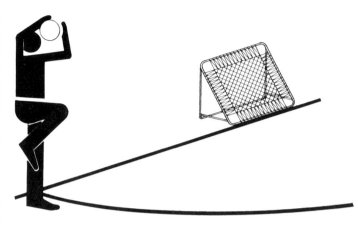

1 The game is played against a framed sprung net

	Standards of play		
	N	C	R
Two-way:	40 × 20m	30–40 × 15–20m	variable
One-way:	—	—	15–20 × 15–20m

Flooring
As the ball should not touch the ground, the game can be played on virtually any surface which is reasonably safe for the players.

Court markings
Lines should be 50mm wide and preferably white. All lines form part of the area which they mark off.

Equipment and storage
One or two rebound nets are required for tchouk-ball, each consisting of a 900 × 900mm frame measuring 1m diagonally, in the centre of which is a nylon net of 40mm mesh, **1**. These have the appearance of miniature square trampoline inclined at an angle of 60° to the floor, and fold flat for storage.

Internal environment
● Lighting should be treated as for handball. All fittings must be fixed at a high level away from the high rebound of the ball.
● Heating should ideally be 12·5°C.
● Ventilation should be treated as for handball.

Spectators
This game has a growing following in Europe, Asia and South America. There are no special considerations other than the fact spectators should not be sited along base lines.

Sources of reference and further advice
The British Tchouk-ball Association handbook

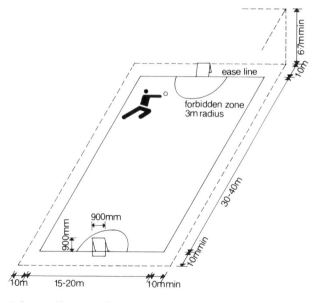

2 Space diagram of two-way tchoukball

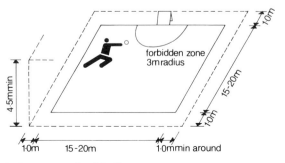

3 One-way tchoukball

21
Tennis: lawn tennis

In some countries, and in the International Tennis Federation rules, the game is known as tennis, the word 'Lawn' being omitted from the title. In Great Britain the official title remains lawn tennis regardless of the surface in use.

Siting
One court, prepared to tournament standard, can be accommodated in a space 36·57 × 18·29 × 9·0m between the draped backcloth netting or canvas on both end walls, **2**.
In a large hall two tennis courts for recreational play may be accommodated in an area 36·5m × 32·0m. Tournament play takes place in the centre of such an arrangement (see **3**). For restricted recreational play in halls of 32m length, which falls well short of the LTA recommended overall length, see the following table and footnote**.

Floor
Flooring must be slip resistant to give players confidence to make their strokes freely and with suitable bounce and spin. If floor sockets are used for post fixings, then these should be designed so as not to interfere with other activities sharing the same space (see Volume 2, Part II, Technical Study **4**). Roll-down portable courts and overlay deck courts are available to order (see Volume 2, Part II, Technical Study **17**).

Court markings
Court markings are noted on **2** and court dimensions are measured to the outside of the white lines. For details see Volume 2, Part II, Technical Study **17**.

Internal environment
● Good even lighting is essential over the whole playing area.

Space

Playing area	Standards of play		
	N	C	R
Length	23·77m	23·77m	23·77m
Width	10·97m	10·97m	10·97m
Clear runback*	6·40**	6·40**	5·49**
	(6·365)		(4·1)
Side run	3·66m	3·66m	3·05m
Between parallel undivided courts	—	4·27m	3·66m
Overall areas			
● One 'centre' court.**	36·57m × 18·29m	36·57m × 18·29m	34·75m × 17·07m
● Two parallel undivided courts	—	36·57m × 33·53m	34·75m** × 31·70m
● Additional parallel courts.	—	+ 15·24m each	+ 14·63m each
● Height	10·67m*** (9·1m)	9·0m	8·0m** (7·6m)

* The LTA advise that the clear runback space must be exclusive of netting or canvas draped 0·300m clear of the back walls to prevent balls rebounding. To allow for this, the LTA therefore recommends that a tournament court space should be 37m long. In a Sports Council large hall, 36·5m long, drapes will reduce the runbacks to about 6·07m (19ft 11in); or slightly more in the earlier 120ft 36·576m, halls.
** The LTA's recommended dimensions exceed the actual clearances (given in brackets) in the Sports Council hall sizes (given in Table II on pp 46–7 in Volume 2), particularly in halls of 32m length, where runbacks are restricted to 4·115m.
*** This is the LTA's recommended height where possible for international competition. The mounting height for TV lighting should also be checked.

1 *Tennis is a major indoor spectator sport. Note the roll-down surface, low ball arrester netting, hospitality boxes at both ends, and the newly developed freestanding net support system which, it is claimed, holds the net taut without need for adjustment between matches. Details are obtainable from the LTA or TUS. Photo: Area Promotional Facilities and Le-Roye Productions Ltd*

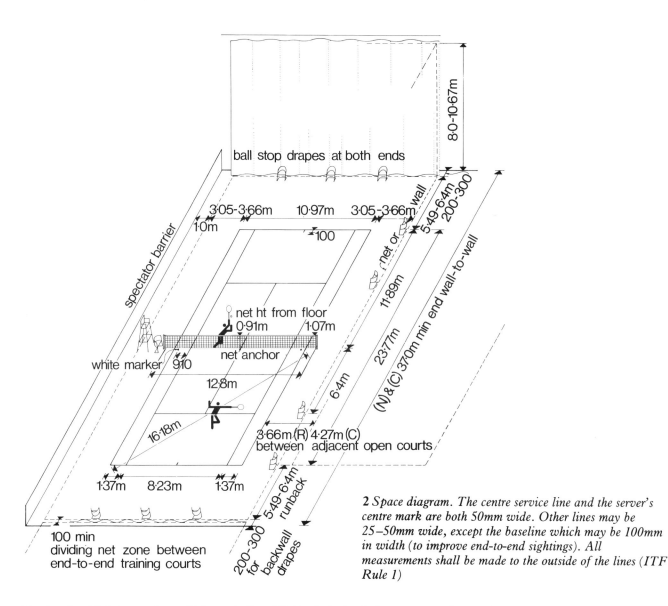

ball stop drapes at both ends

8·0-10·67m

spectator barrier

3·05-3·66m   10·97m   3·05-3·66m   5·49-6·4m   200-300

1·0m   100   net or wall

11·89m

net ht from floor   0·91m   1·07m

23·77m   (N) & (C) 370m min end wall-to-wall

white marker   9·10

net anchor

12·8m   6·4m

16·18m

3·66m (R) 4·27m (C)
between adjacent open courts

1·37m   8·23m   1·37m

5·49-6·4m runback

200-300 for backwall drapes

100 min
dividing net zone between
end-to-end training courts

2 *Space diagram. The centre service line and the server's centre mark are both 50mm wide. Other lines may be 25–50mm wide, except the baseline which may be 100mm in width (to improve end-to-end sightings). All measurements shall be made to the outside of the lines (ITF Rule 1)*

For levels of lighting, refer to Volume 1, Part IV, Technical Study **14**.

● IAKS recommends a maximum noise level of 45 dB.

Programming and charges
Tennis occupies a great deal of space in proportion to the number of players involved. Therefore it is usually necessary in multi-purpose sports halls to programme it for off-peak periods, early morning, early evening, the weekend (perhaps Sunday afternoon), or late evening.
Charges may relate to club bookings or be organised on an individual basis. As such a large area is occupied, these charges are proportionately high.

Spectator facilities
High-level galleries are suitable for casual watching. For occasions when competitions are staged, mobile retractable seating is normally positioned along one or more sides of the playing area (see Volume 2, Part II, Technical study **12**), **3**.

Critical factors
Draped stop-netting across backwalls of tournament courts/height/floor/sockets/spectator provision.

Sources of reference and advice
The Lawn Tennis Association
International Tennis Federation Rules of Tennis
See also Volume 3, Part II, Technical Study 5

3 *Arrangement of courts in a large hall*

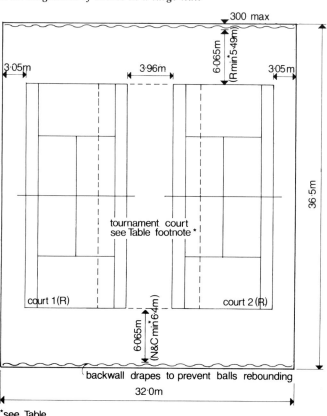

300 max

3·05m   3·96m   6·065m (R min 5·49m)   3·05m

36·5m

tournament court
see Table footnote *

court 1 (R)   court 2 (R)

6·065m (N&C min 6·64m)

backwall drapes to prevent balls rebounding

32·0m

*see Table

22
Trampolining

Siting

Trampolines are sometimes used in pairs and require adequate space around for coaching groups. During synchronised competitions the trampolines must be parallel to each other with a distance of 2m between them, **2**.

A minimum headroom of 8m from bed to ceiling (minimum clear hall height 9·1m) is sought for international regional and sub-regional competitions. For recreational trampolining the absolute minimum safe headroom is 5·5m in halls 6·7m high.

In this ever higher flying sport, hall heights have become the critical factor. The dangers and limitations of decreasing headroom cannot be over-emphasised and are the cause for serious concern, particularly in the planning and design of new halls.

Additional headroom might be gained where frames can be arranged symmetrically beneath parallel roof beams where there is no ceiling or any other obstruction between beams spaced apart sufficiently for the headroom saftey zone **2** to fit in between. Then, the clear headroom can be measured up to the underside of the roof deck supports or other secondary structure. Care must be taken to position this facility clear of curtain net tracks, and to route services trunking, etc, clear of the safety zone. A similar example of this approach can be seen in Data Sheet 3, illustrations **1** and **6**, which features badminton between the beams at The Belgrave Sports Hall, Tamworth, a TUS Development Project.

Space

Trampolines	Standards N	C	R
Length of competition bed	3·6–4·3m	3·6–4·3m	—
Width of competition bed	1·8–2·15m	1·8–2·15m	—
Length of frame*	5·2m (± 100mm)	4·5–5·2m	4·5–5·2m
Width of frame**	3·05m (± 100mm)	2·7–3·05m	2·7–3·05m
Height from floor	1·15m (+ 100mm)	1·05–1·15m	0·95–1·05m
Space around			
Min clear space both ends	3·0m	3·0m	3·0m
Including landing mat min	2·4 × 1·8m	2·4 × 1·8m	2·4 × 1·8m
Min clear space both sides	2·0m	2·0m	2·0m
Distance between pairs	2·0m	2·0m	2·0m
Minimum overall space			
One trampoline	11·2–16* × 7·05m	11·2–16* × 7·05m	10·5–11·2m × 6·7–7·05m
Synchronized pair	11·2–16* × 12·10m	11·2–16* × 12·10m	12 × 12m approx
Height of hall†	7·0–9·1m	7·0–9·1m	6·7m

* Most competitions use the full international size. Latest types of trampoline include spotting decks as an integral part of the framework. These increase the frame by about 5m to approximately 10m long.
** Competition trampolines are now increasingly fitted with additionally wide integral safety sides. Those fitted with removable safety sides can be even wider.
† International Competition Rule 9.1 requires that the interior height of the hall in which trampoline competitions are to take place must be at least 7m (assumed to be the clear floor-to-ceiling height). Experienced trampolinists regularly rise over 6m from the bed (the world record stands at 7·6m from the floor). Performers, at these heights, need at least another 1·5m clearance beneath the ceiling or any obstruction. Also frame heights are tending to rise as standards increase and beds bounce-touch the floor.

Minimum hall heights have therefore become more and more critical to safeguard against accidents and to avoid inhibiting skills and routines, and the development of the sport.

1 *For training and competitions trampolines are now rigged with crash mats and safety sides (see Table footnotes). Mats at both ends can be supported on gymnastic beams or other temporary framework. Latest models are being fitted with hinged leg-frame 'spotting' decks to take crash mats. Photo: The British Trampoline Federation*

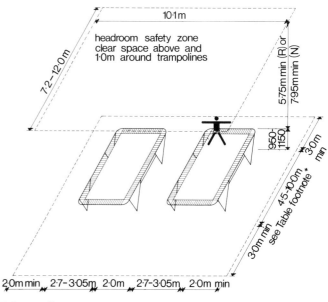

2 *Space diagram*

Flooring

Battened floors should take into account the point loading from the trampoline, which can be very considerable for a top performer bottoming from a height of 6·8m. Recent measurements, quoted by the Scottish Trampoline Association (STA) showed that, assuming an even load through the four points, there would be over a 227kg point load. However, there is much more likely to be uneven pressure onto the floor in excess of 455kg.

The International Trampoline Federation (ITF) competition rules require that gym mats must cover the floor around the trampoline. Thicker landing, or crash, mats must be used at the ends of the frame. It is becoming a necessary practice also to line the floor beneath the trampoline with 100mm thick crash mats to safeguard high fall performers who can bottom the bed onto the floor.

Avoid steps and thresholds. The trampoline on roller stands is heavy to manhandle, particularly for young performers if staff are unavailable.

Walls and circulation

All doorways en route from storage to the place of use should be wide and high enough for the easy and direct movement of trampolines on roller stands. In TSOO the recommended clear height of all access openings is given as 2·7m (2·3m absolute minimum depending on type of equipment).

Ceiling-level equipment

A safety rig is required over each training trampoline, securely fixed to the roof or ceiling structure, **3**, at a minimum height of 5·4m from the floor. Where ceiling heights are restricted, the overhead support may have to be placed to one side of the headroom safety zone, **2**. When setting the overhead rig, the side ropes should ideally form an angle of 45° with the performer's torso when standing on the trampoline. The BTA advise that in 9·1m high halls, about 14m would be necessary between the pulleys of a rig. The double pully must not be placed against a wall since the operator will be lifted off the floor while arresting the performer's downward motion. For two adjacent trampolinists using overhead training rigs an overall space of approx 30m is required: considerably wider than the competition space given in the table and shown in **2**. For futher details consult specialist equipment suppliers.

Internal environment

● Lighting should avoid glare at high level

● A temperature of 12·5°C should be adequate. Equipment must be avoided within the exercise headrooms.

Storage

A regulation size trampoline 2·74 × 4·6 × 0·99m will fold into a space approximately 2·74 × 0·23m high on roller stands, **4**.

A maximum size trampoline will fold into a space approximately 3·5 × 0·23 × 2·25m high on roller stands, but additional turning circle space must be allowed, in the equipment store layout, to park and readily remove a particular trampoline. Avoid overlapped storage which causes trampolines to become entangled.

Storage is also required for surrounding safety mats up to 100m thickness (see floors). Specialist equipment suppliers should be consulted for further details. See also Volume 2, Part II, Technical Study **4**, regarding storage access openings.

Critical factors

Height at all standards. Floor mats. 'Spotting' facilities and the length of frames.

Sources of reference

British Trampoline Federation Ltd
Scottish Trampoline Association
For futher advice also consult the International Trampoline Federation and the UK governing bodies

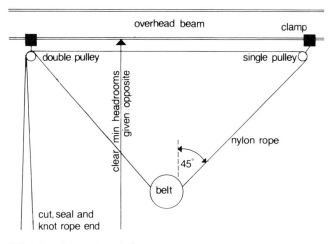

3 *Setting the overhead rig*

4 *Foldaway trampoline storage*

23
Tug-of-war

Siting
Indoor tug-of-war events generally take place on a secure mat thick enough to protect competitors from injury in the event of collapse, **1**. A space at least 35m long is needed which restricts indoor competition to large sports halls, **2**. Practice and club pulls can fit diagonally into medium halls and recreational pulls into small halls.

Floor markings
Competitions take place on a thick rigid mat of interlocking sections which has a slip-resistant under-surface, and is heavy enough to remain stable without being tethered to the floor, **3**.
Three floor markings only are used for indoor tug-of-war. The centre of the markings indicates the centre of the mat and the others are 4m on either side. Markings are placed directly on to the floor between six marker posts, **2**.

Rope
The rope is not less than 100mm and not more than 123mm in circumference and about 16–20m long.

Storage
Storage will be required for the rope coil drum, marker posts and a sectional mat on trolleys.

Sources of reference and advice
The Tug of War Association

1 *Photo: Lee Valley Regional Park Authority/Picketts Lock Centre*

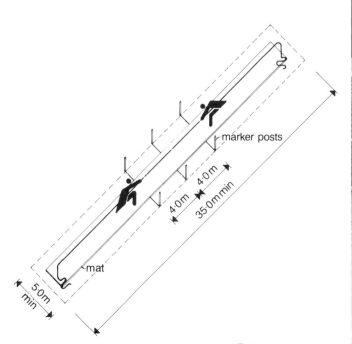

2 *Space diagram*

3 *Note the interlocking device. Photo: Mark Shearman*

24
Volleyball and mini-volleyball

Siting

Provided the court has a 2–3m minimum of extra space all round, this game can be played anywhere in a common sports space. In its equipment and facilities guide, The English Volleyball Association recommends that sports halls should be wide enough to accommodate a volleyball court widthways, to maximise the use of floor space and to allow other activities to take place at the same time. That arrangement is possible in all standard hall sizes except the small widths (see Volume 2, Part II, Technical Study **4**). Courts placed thus could be used for play at all levels except international which are placed centrally within seating. Volleyball is also very popular with disabled players, **3**.

Space

Playing area	Standards of play				
	⚭	N	C	R	♿
Length	18·0m	18·0m	do	do	
Width	9·0m	9·0m	do	do	
Backline clear space	8·0m**	3·0m	3·0m	2·0min***	
Sideline clear space	5·0m**	3·0m	2–3·0m***	2·0min***	
Officials space additional one side	—	+ 2·0m	+ 2·0m	—	
Overall area	34 × 19m	24 × 17m	24 × 16–17m	min 22 × 13m	
Clear unobstructed Height	12·5m	9·0m	7·0min	6·7*	

* Below 7·0m minimum recommended by the EVA. Suitable for mini-volleyball with a lower net height
** Also for final rounds of the World Championships and similar competitions unless a special concession is made by the International Volleyball Federation (IVBF)
*** 3·0m for outdoor courts

When volleyball is set out in small halls, so that other activities may take place at the same time (thus also avoiding very high charges having to be made for volleyball) the court should be placed to one end allowing space for martial arts and table tennis etc behind curtaining (see Volume 2, Part II, Technical Study **4**, **15**, and other illustrations).
Mini-volleyball is played on a full size court but with a lower net level, **2**.

Floor

The EVA offers the following advice about flooring. The main aim in volleyball is to prevent the ball touching the floor, but on many occasions players will come into contact with the floor when playing the ball. A basic technique of volleyball is the forward dive recovery shot which results in the player landing on his chest and sliding forward. This means:
● The floor must be smooth and non-abrasive but not slippery
● The surface must be splinterproof
● Where floor fittings are inserted they must be flush-fitting
● Channels for sliding partitions should not run across volleyball courts
● Cork tiles, tarmacadam and felt type finishes are totally unsuitable for halls where volleyball is played
● The EVA requires that net posts be of the floor-socket type

1 *Photo: Sports Council for Wales*

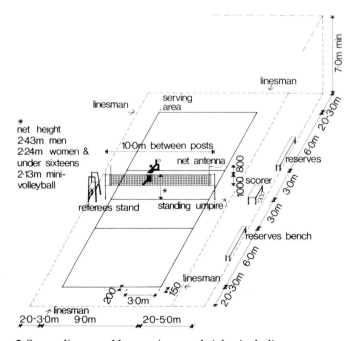

2 *Space diagram. Note various net heights including mini-volley ball*

and not held down by weights. For socket details consult equipment suppliers.
● Roll-down portable courts can be obtained to order and size (see Volume 2, Part II, Technical Study **17**).

48

Court markings

The lines, 5cm wide, are included in the area of the court and the colour code for volleyball lines is green (however to obtain sufficient contrast with the floor, other colours are acceptable). For court marking techniques see Volume 2, Part II, Technical Study **17**. Portable roll-down courts are marked in white.

Spectator facilities

Volleyball is a highly popular spectator sport in most countries of the world and especially in Europe. Spectator facilities should be along the side of the hall so that play in both halves of the court can be watched.

Internal environment

• Background heating only is required. The IVBF rule requires 10°C minimum for players, but if spectators are to be accommodated, a higher level of at least 15°C is required.

• Natural or mechanical ventilation is equally suitable.

• EVA recommends that the hall should be enclosed and artificial lighting used. Sports halls which make use of natural lighting are often very difficult to play in under certain weather conditions. Lights should be protected so that they are not broken by balls during play and hanging lights are not acceptable. An intensity of 500–1500 lux at 1m above the floor is recommended for internationals. Lighting must be phased to avoid strobe.

• Walls and ceiling should be designed to reduce reverberation time. This game is noisy and should not be played near quieter games such as badminton. It is not affected by other sports.

Storage

Storage is required for the rolled-up net, which measures approximately 1m × 0·300m in diameter, posts and net

3 *Amputees' volleyball. Photo: The Northamptonshire Chronicle*

height-gauge. For matches storage will also be required for officials' tables, control equipment and a referee's stand approximately 0·6 × 0·75 × 2·1m high.

Critical considerations

Adequate height/siting in small halls/noise/floor condition.

Sources of reference

The UK governing bodies for volleyball
The International Volleyball Federation

25 Weight-lifting contests

Siting

It is important to draw a distinction between the differing spaces for weight-lifting and weight training. The latter requires an exclusive space, the weight training room, which has been described and illustrated in Volume 2, Part II, Technical Study **5**, p 52.

Whilst the British Amateur Weight Lifting Association (BAWLA) advises that weight training rooms should contain a weight-lifting area, this Data Sheet is about competition weight-lifting spaces which can be sited in a common sports area, hall or arena.

This sport could be accommodated anywhere in which its portable equipment could be installed and for this reason, theatres and public halls where a stage exists, have been popular venues.

The basic requirement is for a competition lifting platform as shown in **2**. An additional warm-up area or adjacent weight-training room is an advantage. For national, international and world competitions consult the BAWLA and relevant competition organisations for minimum space dimensions.

Floor

Having established that this sport should not be confused with weight training, it should be emphasised that weight-lifting requires a non-slip platform over a floor sufficiently robust to take the impact of weights dropped on to the surface. The platform itself is constructed to reduce and spread the impact on the structure. The non-slip nature of the top surface is, essential. It is usually unpolished plain wood. Adjacent areas for warm-up and spare weights must be protected. A level, slip-resistant floor is also required.

Internal environment

● A background temperature of 10–13°C is recommended for this sport

● Good ventilation is essential

● Noise control is important in this sport as a quiet environment, free from background noise, is essential for concentrated lifting.

Equipment

In addition to the platform an international 200kg set of weights is required for all competitions. Tables for officials, competitors' chairs or benches, a score board, public address system and warm-up area mats will also be required.

Storage

After use weights should be stored clear of the floor area, either in an adjacent weight training room or in lockable storage racks. This precaution is as much for security as tidyness.

1 *Photo: Colorsport*

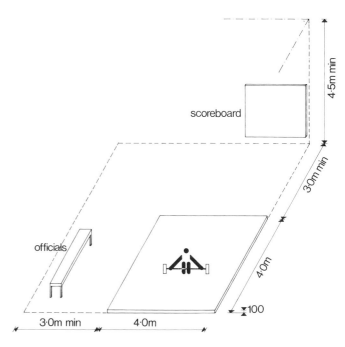

2 *Space diagram of competition area. The special platform can be raised on staging if that improves spectator viewing. At floor level line markings of other sports can be distracting to lifters and should be covered by thin matting. For TV presentations a backcloth curtain can be placed behind the platform to screen the competitors warm-up and waiting area. The scoreboard is then brought forward*

Competitors
In major championships, ten competitors and two reserves are allowed from each team or country.

Spectators
Seating should be allowed for 500 spectators at championship events and up to 2000 at internationals.

Critical factors
Noise control/ventilation/floor protection

Source of reference
British Amateur Weight-Lifting Association

26
Wrestling

Siting
In a multi-sports centre wrestling training is likely to share a space suitable for other 'combat sports' and other smaller space activities. See Volume 2, Part II, Technical Study **0** for use of practice halls.

Squad training and the training of technical officials and coaches requires a training hall which can take at least one 11m × 11m mat. A further safety area of 1m all round is advised, or failing that, the walls of the training hall should be protected by a suitable foam-backed material up to 2m from the ground.

For national and international matches a mat 10–12m square with a clear space of 1–2m all round must be provided. National and regional championships require two, three and occasionally four mats to be set out in the same hall, **3, 4**.

Space

Combat area	Standards ⊛	N	C	R
Length	12·0m	10·0–12·0m*	10·0/11·0m	min 10·0m
Width	12·0m	10·0–12·0m*	10·0/11·0m	min 10·0m
Surrounding space	3·0m		min 1·0m	
Officials sides		min 2·0m		
Other sides		min 1·0m		
Overall area				
One mat**	18 × 18m	14·0–16·0* × 12·0–14·0m*	12·0/13·0m square	min 10·0 × 10·0m
Height		6·7m***	4·5m min	3·5m min

* In all international competitions and for World, European and continental championships a 9·0m diameter mat is obligatory. For other tournaments an 8·0m diameter mat is authorized

** See **4** for the overall area of two, three and four competition mats

*** Allowing possibly for a raised platform

Equipment
At tournaments an electric scorer/timer should be provided for each mat plus two separate stop watches for time out.

Competitors
International matches require residential accommodation for about 30 people. National and regional championships attract between 60 to 300 competitors, some requiring accommodation.

Spectators
Wrestling is not a great spectator sport, and spectator attendance for international, national or regional matches rarely exceeds 2000.

Storage
Storage space will be required for timing and scoring equipment and for competition mats.

Sources of reference
British Amateur Wrestling Association

1 *Photo: William Baxter*

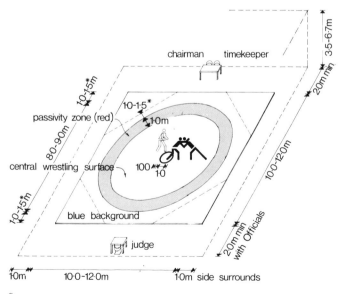

chairman   timekeeper

passivity zone (red)

central wrestling surface

blue background

judge

*minimum protection surface of same thickness as Mat

10–1·5*m   80–9·0m   10–1·5*m   10–1·5*   1·0m   100   1·0

3·5–6·7m   20m min   10·0–12·0m   2·0m min with Officials

1·0m   10·0–12·0m   1·0m side surrounds

2 *Space diagram. Professional Wrestling uses a raised ring similar to boxing, and is quite unlike free-style and Greco-Roman (amateur) wrestling*

3 *Competition mats. Photo: William Baxter*

4 *Dimensions of multi ring layouts. For Olympic Games combat four rings are required on a single raised platform with sides angled at 45° to the floor. Three or four mats arranged in a 31 × 31m square pattern would fit a large size sports hall*

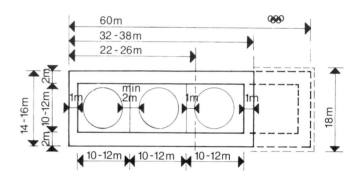

Part II Indoor exclusive space activities

27
Athletics and indoor training facilities

Introduction

Concern over the lack of facilities available for athletes to train and compete indoors has been expressed in many quarters for a considerable length of time. The unreliability of the British climate means that competitors in technical and explosive events may not be able to train outdoors for long periods without considerable discomfort and in many cases an unacceptable risk of injury. Indoor provision is therefore essential, and must become more widely available, **1–3**.

The explosion in the provision of indoor sports halls and sport and leisure centres has led to considerable expansion in many indoor games, as well as to indoor versions of outdoor games. This has not, however, been reflected in athletics. Some of the reasons for this may be:

- The difficulty in programming athletics with other sports
- The specialist requirements for floors, pits, nets, and landing mats
- The relatively large space traditionally required to train relatively small groups of athletics
- The relatively long periods of exclusive use of facilities traditionally required by athletes to carry out training programmes
- The need for indoor athletics training during the winter when most sports centres have their highest demands for evening usage in other activities

While the situation has been disappointing in the past, there are indications that some facility providers are now considering the needs of athletes and good examples are outlined later.

The Sports Council and the Amateur Athletic Association, in conjunction with the British Amateur Athletic Board, are to publish a technical booklet which will draw attention to the needs of athletics in indoor facilities and to suggest ways in which such facilities might be provided without unacceptably high cost to the provider. This Data Sheet and Data Sheet 28 precede the booklet which should be referred to for further details and technical advice.

Types of facilities

Facilities for indoor athletics consist of two main categories. These are:

- *Training facilities* which are usually purpose-built or adaptions of existing sports halls intended for some limited competitive use.
- *Facilities for competition* which not only provide for the full range of competitive athletic disciplines, but will have spectator provision associated with them. Such facilities form the of Data Sheet 28.

Background information: training facilities

The provision of training facilities for athletes indoors (but with some limited competitive use) need not be the expensive provision of 200m banked tracks. Many events can be simulated indoors for training purposes if the brief for the facility is thought out in advance and includes consideration of the

1 *An early covered training area at Lilleshall Hall National Sports Centre. Photo: Sports Council Publications*

2 *An indoor sprint straight and training area. Photo: Sports Council Publications*

needs of athletes. The providers of sports halls are now encouraged to think of the needs of athletes in the planning stage of sports centres, so this major spectator and participant sport can gain some of the same benefits from indoor provision that other sports have received, **4**.

The Wood Green School sports hall, London Borough of Haringey, **5**, **6**, is a Sports Council prototype scheme for an athletics extension of a school sports hall to provide one L-shaped area capable of use for a wide range of school and community sports besides athletics training indoors. It opened in February 1980, and is the first facility of its kind in this country. It is situated opposite one of the top athletic club tracks, and together they form the New River Sports Centre. The hall is a joint-provision facility: it is located on a school site but is managed by the borough recreation department.

The Borough of Gateshead has also produced an interesting project, which is described later and is illustrated in **8** and **9**.

Training areas in converted buildings
Conversions of smaller buildings which can only accommodate a 160m or 200m track, but without the space to provide the seating which would make them into full competitive facilities, should be considered as regional training centres. The technical specifications for these should be the same as for competitive facilities but lacking the spectator provision. On a smaller scale a training area which has some competitive potential has been provided at the National Recreation Centre at Crystal Palace. This area, which has been created by enclosing the void under a walkway, is 80m long by approximately 14m wide (the width varies due to pillars). These dimensions, which might well be copied elsewhere, allow ample length for sprint training and jumping pits have also been provided. Provision for the high jump and throwing events is limited.

If such facilities were being specially built, some part of the roof should be high enough to accommodate pole-vault training as described later.

A separate area for weight training should be provided and a netted area for throwing practice, **6**. Technical specifications for this are given below.

Athletics training in existing sports halls
Existing halls can be used for athletics training if athletes and management are prepared to exercise some degree of compromise. Where floors are not suitable to accept spiked shoes, athletes may train in 'flats'. Halls of 32m and 36·5m length can provide useful sprint and hurdle practice and high jumps can be performed on to landing mats, **4**. Long and triple jumps can also be practised on to mats, as long as these can be secured and prevented from sliding. Archery and cricket nets can be strengthened and adapted for throwing practice with some care. Light roll-out strips, of 10–12mm minimum thickness, can be provided at slightly greater cost for practice with spikes. Existing halls might also be adapted and extended, as shown in **5**. An example of an existing large hall used for small scale athletics meetings is the Wycombe Sports Centre where a 50m sprint straight is provided by annexing store rooms on opposite sides of the hall (see Volume 2, Technical Study 4, p 50).

Purpose-built training facilities
When contemplating a new sports hall development, providers could consider certain adaptions which would make the facility useful as an athletics training area, as well as making it suitable for other sports and recreational activities, **7**. It can also be built in extendable phases, as in the case of Wood Green School, London, **5** and Gateshead Sports Stadium, **8**, **9**. Impressive West German examples include the L-shaped

3 *A demountable, portable, banked track. Photo: Ron Davies of ARENA, W. Vancouver*

4 *School atheletics practice in sports hall, Belgrave Centre, Tamworth. Photo: David Butler*

training shed at Bochum opened in 1977 and the flat indoor 200m track at Dusseldorf which is also used for competitions.

This may be achieved in a number of ways and requires the following points to be taken into consideration:

Planning
Athletics is a club-based sport and few towns or districts have more than one club which would require an indoor training base. For this reason only one specially-adapted facility is likely to be required per district. Districts which have leisure and recreation development plans including more than one sports centre or hall could designate one of these to be developed or adapted for use as the local athletics training facility. Location adjacent to, or near, the main athletics track would be advantageous. Opportunities for joint provision and dual use should, of course, be considered as more economic forms of provision, **5, 6.**

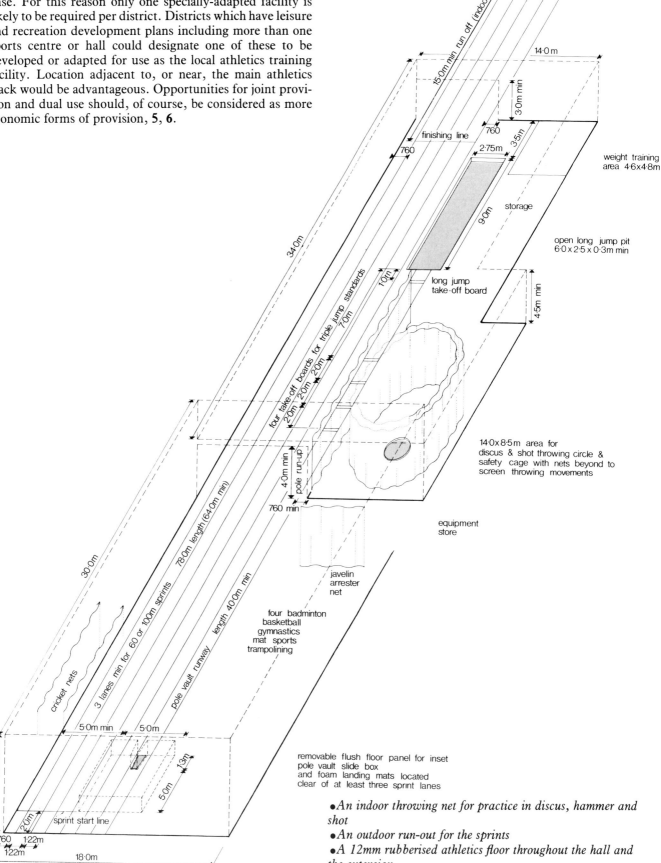

weight training
area 4·6 x 4·8m

storage

open long jump pit
6·0 x 2·5 x 0·3m min

long jump
take-off board

14·0 x 8·5m area for
discus & shot throwing circle &
safety cage with nets beyond to
screen throwing movements

equipment
store

javelin
arrester
net

four badminton
basketball
gymnastics
mat sports
trampolining

removable flush floor panel for inset
pole vault slide box
and foam landing mats located
clear of at least three sprint lanes

5 *Space diagram of Wood Green school and community sports and athletics training hall. The sports hall is a standard 32 × 17 × 7·6m hall but with several interesting additional features:*
• *An extra 'leg' which allows a 60m sprint to be run indoors*
• *Built-in long and triple jump pits*

• *An indoor throwing net for practice in discus, hammer and shot*
• *An outdoor run-out for the sprints*
• *A 12mm rubberised athletics floor throughout the hall and the extension.*
If high jump is included then the width of the hall needs to be a minimum of 23m, with jump landing mats on the clear side of the hall and the fan shaped run up zone overlapping the sprint straights. If this overlapping is to be avoided the hall needs to be 32m wide. (Architects: London Borough of Haringey)

Siting

Where ancillary halls for projectile or other sports are to be provided in conjunction with main sports halls, these can be aligned to provide an acceptable sprint length. These ancillary areas should also contain any landing areas (except for high jump) or pits etc, **5**.

Assuming the kind of spaces provided by the addition of an ancillary hall to a normal sports hall in the way described above, the use of the hall can be maximised by laying out the activities to enable the greatest number of events to be practised simultaneously. Some suggestions are shown in **8** and **9**.

Floor surface

Surfaces for indoor athletics vary little from those available for outdoor all-weather tracks. Principal differences occur in the method of installation rather than in the actual materials used. Timber, sheet rubber and plastic materials are used as opposed to in-situ alternatives available for outdoors. The substrates should be laid level and the surface bonded to it. Factors particularly important to athletes are rebound resilience (person/surface), stiffness, friction and wear. In addition, it is essential that the surface is sufficiently thick for the appropriate spikes for training.

Athletes prefer to train in spiked shoes, thus simulating track conditions more accurately. Indoor spikes are a maximum of 6mm in length and therefore a synthetic floor material of at least 10mm and preferably 12mm depth is required. Where an 'indoor' material is provided care must be taken to ensure that its chemical composition includes the same form of spike inhibiting compound contained in outdoor surfaces.

'Outdoor' surfaces normally have greater traction than other indoor sports floors and therefore may not be suitable for some indoor games where a degree of slip is necessary.

A polymeric or rubber floor material of adequate thickness is necessarily more expensive than tile or wooden floors. However, such a surface has advantages for other sports, some of which are:

- Greater resilience giving greater comfort to sports participants in a wide variety of games
- Lines may be painted directly onto the surface
- There may be safety advantages.

Against this must be set the possible problem of greater susceptibility to indentation from point-loading, a factor making the use of chairs for social and arts functions more difficult. This may cause the facility to lose a degree of multi-purposeness. Roll-down synthetic fibre textile indoor athletics surfaces being developed in Scandinavia might help to overcome this dilemma. Problems of wear and tear from the throwing events should be also carefully considered (see the section on netting below).

A number of products are currently on the market which could adequately cater for the requirements of athletics. The Sports Council and the Rubber Plastics Research Association are engaged in a research project which will hopefully result in British Standards for sports floors, for a wide variety of uses and purposes.

Up-to-date information on the progress of the research is available from the Technical Unit for Sport at the Sports Council. A list of surface manufacturers is available from the Sports Council Information Centre.

In-situ jumping pits

Jumping pits are required for *long and triple jump* and landing areas for high jump and pole vault are also necessary, **5, 8, 9**.

- The insertion of a jumping pit into a sports hall floor is shown in **10**. The important consideration in such a facility is its location to avoid areas where a change in floor characteristics might produce 'dead spots' in areas critical to other

6 *The sprint straight extension leg with the throwing cage bay on the left and the adapted hall in the background. Photo: Tommy Hindley*

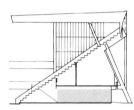

7 *At the Meadowbank Sports Centre, Edinburgh, the west wing of the indoor centre extends for 134m on two floors under the athletics stadium. The ground floor has a dual function. When an event is being staged in the stadium it provides a huge foyer for spectators entering the stand and at other times, it becomes an indoor training area with a 4-lane 110m sprint straight and a double height section for pole vaulting. (Architect: City Architect, Edinburgh)*

sports eg under basketball goals. The best location is in the annexed area created by an adjacent ancillary hall **5**. Being free from wind resistance, run-ups need only be in one direction and more than one pit will rarely be needed. If more than one is provided, they should be located side-by-side with about 1·5–2m between. To avoid dazzling athletes on the run-up, there should be no windows in the wall at the end of the pit. The handles for lifting out the pit cover should fit flush to the floor surface and it is probably preferable to use socketed lifting keys, rather than have the handles folding into the floor.

Some way of securing the floor over the pits will probably be needed. Take-off boards should be reversible and fit flush to the existing floor surface both in use and when stored.

A design for reversible take-off boards and pole vault boxes is available in the UK.

- The use of foam landing areas, **4**, means that *high jump* training can be held in the body of the main hall rather than along the sprint straight. The main difficulty will be the storage of landing areas but since they may also be used for gymnastics, storage may not be too much of a problem.

- The obvious need for *pole vault* training is for a clear height over and around the landing area. For this reason, it may be better to locate the pit in the body of the main hall at the start/finish of the sprint straight **5, 11**, where sufficient height should exist. If the pit is located in the annexed area, a clear headroom of 8·9m is required over the whole area of the pit and over a 1·5m area surrounding it. A minimum height of 4·5m above the runway is also particularly important so that the athletes' perspective is not disturbed and to avoid

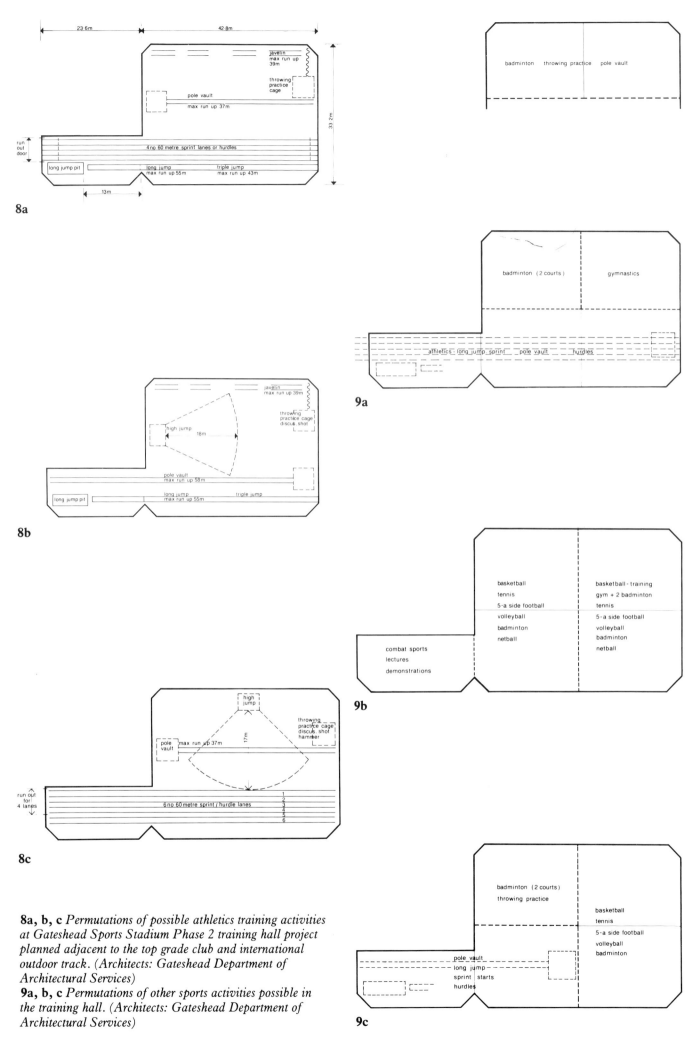

8a

8b

8c

9a

9b

9c

8a, b, c *Permutations of possible athletics training activities at Gateshead Sports Stadium Phase 2 training hall project planned adjacent to the top grade club and international outdoor track. (Architects: Gateshead Department of Architectural Services)*

9a, b, c *Permutations of other sports activities possible in the training hall. (Architects: Gateshead Department of Architectural Services)*

causing a premature lowering of the pole during the approach, through the opening into the taller main hall, which will affect the plant into the take-off box and thus have a detrimental effect on technique and height.

The pole vault take-off box must be inset into the floor. The same considerations apply to this as to the pit covers and take-off boards although on a smaller scale. To avoid a 'dead' spot in the floor the inset should completely fill the 'box' without leaving a hollow. Pole vault stands may present some storage problems, as they are longer than most sports hall equipment. The siting of the long/triple jump and pole vault run-ups and landing areas should ensure that at least three sprinting lanes are available.

Netting for throwing event practice

Throwing events must be practised in a fully enclosed netted area, **6**. Such an area would need specially strengthened and probably double-layered netting, capable of stopping a discus, shot, hammer or javelin thrown from fairly short range. Equipment manufacturers should be consulted about the safety design of such a netting system. The suggested shape seeks to avoid square corners, which could be areas of weakness. The netting should overlap so there is no danger of openings through which the implement is likely to eject. The curtain run should lock into place when fully extended to avoid accidental opening. The netting should be thoroughly checked on a regular basis.

The throwing circles, for the three throwing events, have slightly different dimensions and characteristics, eg the shot has a stop board. Only one portable circle should be provided and its dimensions varied by inserts of the correct diameter. Where the cage is adjacent to the sprint lanes and run-ups the throwing bay should be screened by sightline curtains to avoid cross-distractions, **5**.

The problem of accommodating the javelin is rather more complex. The practice implement should certainly not be pointed, but every effort should be made to maintain its balance. The event also requires a run-up for which the curtain should be open at one end, **5**.

This netting cage, if properly designed, should be absolutely safe, but it is suggested that a Health and Safety Officer should be consulted before it is used and warning notices placed around its perimeter. If at all possible, the javelin throws should be performed away from the sprint straight and high-jump area and preferably at a blank wall.

If the javelin net is placed in the main hall area, there may be a problem of wear and tear on the floor since the stopping action as the thrower launches the javelin may damage the floor. This also happens with the pole vault.

Storage

A considerable amount of equipment not usually associated with sports halls will need storage and additional storage space will be needed. Readers should also consult the remarks about storage in Table 2 of the following Data Sheet. Throwing implements should be stored in a locked cupboard. Starting blocks and hurdles (which should be capable of folding) can be stored in a standard storage area, but pole vault stands and high-jump and pole vault landing areas may need special storage arrangements. It is estimated that an additional 20m² of storage would be needed for athletics purposes, but this should be carefully assessed.

Ancillary facilities

As a club sport, athletics would probably not require any additional specialist facilities and athletes would probably produce a good return in bar and catering areas. A club room which would be normally provided in such a facility would be additionally useful for committee and coaching discussions.

10 *Long and triple jump pit inset into floor at Wood Green School. Photo: Tommy Hindley*

11 *Pole vaulting headroom can be critical in small or medium size halls of only 7·6m height. Photo: Tommy Hindley*

Weight training area

A weight training area is absolutely essential since many athletes train extensively with weights in winter. A schedule of athletes' weight training equipment is given on p 64. Changing areas should be large enough to accommodate a training squad of 50–100 persons changing at the facility before and after a run, as well as those training on site. This would improve the club atmosphere on a training night.

Programming

The programming of any facility is the responsibility of the manager and the managing authority and demand for a wide range of activities has to be balanced in order to avoid conflict and optimise use.

Where the facility is specifically designed with athletics in mind this should not affect any of the other activities. It would mean, however, that large blocks of time might need to be subtracted from the programme. During the winter, athletic clubs might require two-evenings use of the facility for all or part of those evenings. To balance this, off-peak time at weekends or during the day-time, might be discussed as alternatives. The final arrangements would be for negotiation between clubs and managers, but it is hoped that the latter would show some sympathy in undertaking the needs of athletic clubs, and the purposes of planning a specialist facility.

Source of further reference

AAA/SC forthcoming publication *Facilities for indoor athletics*

61

28
Athletics: facilities for competition

Background

Since 1862, this sport has been forced to rely upon non-purpose built facilities to stage indoor competitions. Between the wars, for example, a demountable track was installed within the Wembley Arena (then the Wembley Pool), and at the now defunct Harringay ice rink. After this, a number of other sites, mainly owned by the RAF, were used before a permanent home for an international athletics track was found at RAF Cosford, **1**. On the European continent and in North America there are increasing numbers of indoor track arenas, **2**.

The search for additional competitive venues continues and a number of large redundant buildings have been investigated. These include numerous aircraft hangars, two unused railway stations at Leith, Scotland (see Volume 2, Part III, TS **2**) and at Crystal Palace, London, and a former exhibition hall. Unbuilt projects for new arenas include those for Snow Hill Birmingham, GLC at Thamesmead, London Borough of Barnet at Copthall Stadium, Essex Sports Centre, Redbridge, and at Sandwell in the West Midlands.

A strategy for the provision of major competitive facilities has been produced by the AAA Indoor Development Committee and includes the provision of four major competitive venues, the first of which should be in London. In the medium and long term respectively, Birmingham and Leeds or Manchester will require such facilities and there is also a need for an indoor arena in Scotland, preferably sited in Edinburgh. Currently, the Sports Council and GLC are engaged in a feasibility study for the National Indoor (multi-purpose) Arena, whilst at the NEC Birmingham another exhibition hall is being built to stage indoor athletics amongst other sports events. The Scottish proposals have been mentioned above.

The technical and design requirements of a major indoor athletics arena are outlined below, based on the joint work of the AAA and TUS.

The European Athletic Association specifies the following requirements for indoor events.

The arena

The arena shall be covered and heated and shall consist of a track circuit, a sprint straight, runways for the four jumps and a site for shot putt.

Nature of tracks

The track and runways shall be surfaced with wood or such other material allowing the normal use of short spiked shoes. The number of spikes shall comply with IAAF rule 142 (4).

1 *Six lane tracks are now being developed for European indoor championships, whilst the UK has to make do with only one four lane banked track at RAF Cosford. Photo: Sports Surfaces International Ltd*

2 *1980 European Championship track at Sindelfingen, West Germany. The 1982 Budapest track will have six lanes. Photo: Michael Schmidt*

Sprint track
The sprint straight shall have at least six lanes, the width of each shall be 1·22m. The extension beyond the finishing line shall be at least 1·5m.

Hurdle races
●For the men's event the 50m hurdles shall include four hurdles, the height of which shall be 1·06m. There shall be 13·72m from the starting line to the first hurdle, 9·14m between the hurdles and 8·86m from the last hurdle to the finish line.
The men's 60m hurdles shall include 5 hurdles the height of which shall be 1·06m. There shall be 13·72m from the starting line to the first hurdle, 9·14m between the hurdles and 9·72m from the last hurdle to the finish line.

The circuit track
One lap of the track shall measure not less than 160m nor more than 200m in length. Each bend shall be not less than 35m in length and banked at an angle of not less than 10°, nor more than 18°. Each straight shall be not less than 35m. Where there is no raised border, the measurement shall be taken 20cm outward from the inner edge of the track. The track shall be not less than 4m nor more than 6·10m in width, and shall include 4 lanes at least.

3 *Space diagram showing a 200m lap track surrounding a sprint and hurdles straight and jump run ups. The broken lines crossing the track indicates the recent European development of a clothoid banking transition from the straights into each bend and down again. In effect the flat straight continues into the bend on the inside lane, whilst on the outside lane the banking starts before the bend, as seen in* **2**. *This is said to ease the transition for the athlete and overcomes humps which otherwise occur*

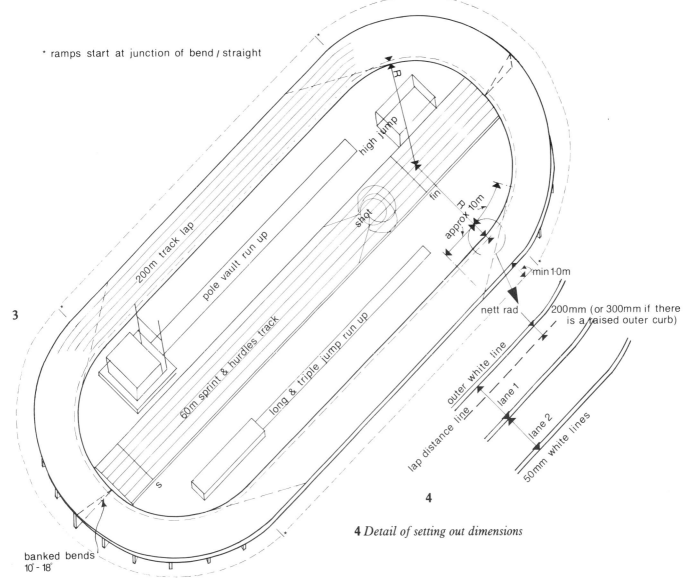

* ramps start at junction of bend / straight

200m track lap

pole vault run up

60m sprint & hurdles track

long & triple jump run up

high jump

shot

fin

approx 10m

min 1·0m

nett rad

200mm (or 300mm if there is a raised outer curb)

outer white line

lap distance line

lane 1

lane 2

50mm white lines

banked bends
10° - 18°

3

4

4 *Detail of setting out dimensions*

Table 1 Alternative dimensions for indoor athletics tracks

Length of track straight[a]	Length of bend[b]	Radius of bend[r]	Overall area required [o/a]	Space for sprint straight[ss]
200m maximum lap				
35m min*	65m	20·491m	91·2 × 56·2m = 5122m²	(75·98)
50m**	50m	15·716m	96·63 × 46·63m = 4506m²	(81·44)
52·248m**	47·752m	15·0m	97·45 × 45·2m = 4404m²	(82·25)
65m	35m min*	10·941m	102·08 × 37·08m = 3785m²	(86·88)
160m minimum lap				
35m min*	45m	14·124m		(63m approx)
40m	40m	12·532m		(65m approx)
45m	35m min*	10·941m		(67m approx)

Notes:

a: A sample range of alternative proportions, based on European Athletic Association regulation minimum dimensions*. The AAA and EAA preferred proportions are the lines noted**. The 35m min bend may become unacceptable if the 200m lap is standardised for competitions

b: Measured 200m from inside of outer white-line around flat edged track, or 300mm inside a raised border or edge framework

r: The tighter the bend the greater the inclination of the bank, 10–18° maximum. The radius given in this table is the *nett* radius after 200mm has been deducted from the gross radius used to calculate the lengths of bends and straights. The radius must not be rounded down where given to three decimal places

o/a: For a six lane track (6·1m max. width); or deduct 4·2m off lengths and widths for a four lane track. Includes 1·5m (1m min) safety margin outside the track up to boundary with spectator seating

ss: Minimum required 80m i.e. approx 5m for collected start space, plus 60m sprint, plus minimum EAAC regulation 15m run out at finish. Absolute minimum 76m, but then starting space is very tight and finish run-out climbs across the end bank. With 200m tracks a guard rail is necessary to stop sprinters; but for banked 160m laps there is really insufficient length for a sprint straight with run out unless reduced to a 50m sprint event. Alternatively, a section of the bend can be removable, but this poses practical problems in programming sprint and track events

●For the women's event the 50m hurdles shall include four hurdles, the height of which shall be 0·84m. There shall be 13·00m from the starting line to the first hurdle, 8·50m between the hurdles and 11·50m from the last hurdle to the finish line. The women's 60m hurdles shall include 5 hurdles, the height of which shall be 0·84m. There shall be 13·00m from the starting line to the first hurdle, 8·50m between the hurdles and 13·00m from the last hurdle to the finish line.

Runways for the long and triple jump and pole vault
These runways shall be not less than 40m in length and 1·22m in width.

Landing areas for jumps
In the high jump and the pole vault, landing areas shall be in accordance with IAF rules 201 (e) and 3 (d).
In the long jump and the triple jump, they shall measure not less than 6m in length and 2·50m in width and shall consist of not less than 0·30m in depth of wet sand on a synthetic track base.

Putting the shot
The sector shall be 45° but may be reduced by the Technical Delegate to meet local conditions if necessary.

Other technical installations
All other technical installations shall be strictly in accordance with IAAF rules. (*End of EAA specification.*)

Siting and dimensions
A typical layout for tracks and runways is shown in **3**. The proportions of the outer-track straights and bends may vary within the EAA limits, and the optimum and extremes are set out in Table 1 together with the differing overall space required for these variables.
The setting-out line of the lap length is explained in detail in **4**. This inside dimension depends on whether the track has a flat edge line or upstanding raised border.

Flooring
See Data Sheet 27, p 56, for details.

Table 2 Equipment for sports halls and arenas

Indoor starting blocks	6 pairs
Indoor hurdles	24/36 (six per lane)
Hurdles knock over top bar	6
Relay batons	6
Indoor high jump stands	1 set
High jump jumping laths	6
Landing area	1 (Mattress type)
Indoor Pole vault stands	1 set
Pole vault laths	6
Pole vaulting box	1 (Portable, can be let into
Vaulting poles, steel, 11ft	2 floor and removed and
Vaulting poles, steel, 13ft	2 space suitably covered)
Bar lifter	1
Landing area	1 (Mattress type)
Cross bar jointing clip	2
Portable circles for shot putt	
Stop board for shot putt	
Rubber mats for floor protection for shot and weight training	
Indoor discus (rubber) 2·00kg	3
,, ,, ,, 1·75kg	3
,, ,, ,, 1·50kg	3
,, ,, ,, 1·00kg	3
Captive discus 2·00kg	1
,, ,, 1·75kg	1
,, ,, 1·50kg	1
,, ,, 1·00kg	1
Indoor Shot 7·257kg	3
,, ,, 6·25kg	3
,, ,, 5·00kg	3
,, ,, 4·00kg	3
Indoor javelins 800g	3
,, ,, 700g	3
,, ,, 600g	3
,, ,, 500g	3
Running harness	4
ISO Exercisers	2 (To simulate mechanics of athletics under resistance)

Throwing nets
Advice should be sought from the National Association on the provision of landing areas, long jump runways, throwing circles and nets as requirements depend on the type of sports hall being provided.
Where a separate weight training room or area is not provided, the following items should also be included:—

Leg press machine (portable)	1
Squat rack (portable)	1
Bar-bell Kits 300lb (136kg)	1
100lb (45kg)	1
Additional bars, dumb-bell rods and collars	3
Leg Bells	2 pairs
Bar-bell racks	1
Incline board (adjustable)	1
Sarjent jump board	1
Adjustable short bench with bench press stands	1

The AAA and the athletics trade are considering the provision of a sectional 200m track to be made available for use by the UK constituent bodies in competition with visiting teams, or for championship matches. The track would be made so that it could, if necessary, be dismantled and transported in sections, by container lorries to another venue. This would also ease storage at a permanent venue. This is not completely a new idea as the original Earls Court track and the Cosford track, 1, were both sectional. There is also a patented design by an ex-international athlete and designer, Ron Davies, on the market. The runways and 'field pits' are built up on to the main floor level.

Alternatively, insitu cast concrete bends produce a permanent track circuit, but flexibility to use the complete space for other purposes is lost although the costs of moving demountable track are saved. An example is the AAA's recently opened track at RAF Cosford.

Equipment storage
Typical equipment used for an indoor event is listed in Table 2.

Ancillary accommodation and the multi-use arena
For advice consult the Sports Council, who have drawn up a brief for a National Indoor Arena around the requirements of indoor athletics.

Internal environment
Little is currently known in the UK about the environmental requirements for indoor athletics, but it is hoped to include advice in the forthcoming AAA/SC publication, *Facilities for indoor athletics*.

29
Billiards and snooker

Space

Critical dimensions and the shape of the space are shown in **2**. The overall size of a full-sized billiard table is approximately 4m × 2m depending on the particular design. The Billiards and Snooker Control Council has introduced (with World agreement) the 'B and SCC 3·50m standard table' and for the first time, this specifies the actual *playing area* size (3·50m × 1·75m) *within* the cushion faces (in place of the overall table size). The existing table standards will also be valid until at least 2000 AD.

A clear playing space of 2m all round the table is desirable, so that a clear floor space of 8m × 6m is required for actual play. Any seating must be positioned outside this area. If the clear playing space around the table is reduced to the absolute minimum of 1·6m, the total playing area can be reduced to 6·75m × 5m.

Table weight and installation

It should be noted that the weight of a full-size traditionally designed billiard table is approximately 1·5 tonne spread over 8 legs. The cost of delivery and erection of a billiard table depends on the situation and distance to be carried, particularly if the table is to be installed upstairs or in a basement. The best situation is at ground level with good vehicle access.

Siting and layout

Billiards and snooker enthusiasts feel their games cannot be played in a common space used for other activities at the same time and the concentration required for club and championship matches demands that a separate space be provided. For recreational play a bay off a multi-purpose games or social space would be satisfactory, provided that the bay could be cut off from the main space when necessary by means of a folding/sliding partition. Tables have to be plumbed and levelled accurately before use and therefore cannot be moved to make room for other activities.

For championships, exhibition or other special matches it is preferable that only one table be in play at a time, permanently positioned to allow for it to be surrounded by elevated spectators: see below. Other tables are then closed down for the match and room lights turned off or dimmed.

It is best to arrange the tables end-to-end to limit the possible obstruction between players at adjacent tables. Where tables have to be placed side-by-side the minimum spacing apart is given in diagram **2**.

Spectator facilities

Spectator seating, if required, should be provided around at least three sides of one table but sufficiently distant from it to allow ample space for the players **2**. Permanent or removable seating is acceptable.

Flooring

A firm level floor finish is essential for the table to be permanently plumbed absolutely level and to withstand the point loads.

Internal environment

● A background temperature of 15·6°C is desirable and adequate ventilation should also be provided to cope with concentrated smoking.

● As regards lighting a player must be able to judge the relative position of the balls and be confident that his ball runs true. Some modelling of the balls is desirable, but harsh shadows must be avoided. Players should not be troubled by

1 *Lilleshall National Sports Centre. Photo: Roger Price Ltd*

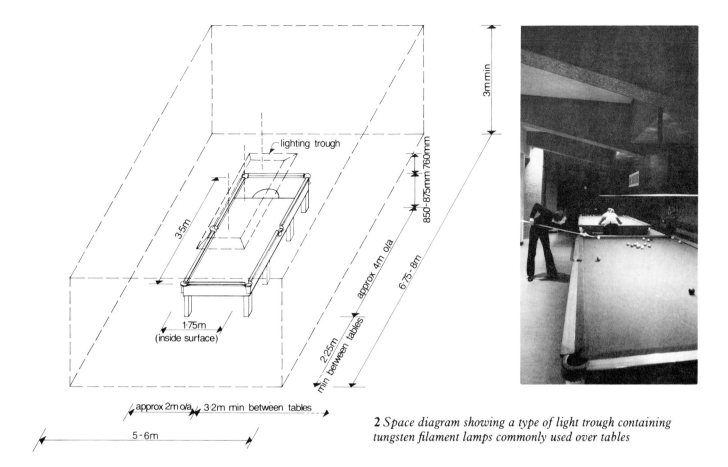

2 *Space diagram showing a type of light trough containing tungsten filament lamps commonly used over tables*

direct or reflected glare or by flicker. Acceptable colour rendering is important for snooker. A bright overall light is needed over each table and natural light is not essential.

For all standards of play, these requirements are satisfied by a suspended lighting trough, **2**, painted white inside and containing three 150 watt tungsten filament lamps separated by baffles to screen them from the players. This produces approximately 375 lux at table level.* These canopy lights are easily serviced. Fluorescent lamps are unacceptable for many reasons. Specialist suppliers of billiard lighting units should be consulted.

It should be noted that modern billiard shades weigh approximately 27·2 kg and therefore require strong ceiling fixtures in order to avoid the risk of collapse and damage to the expensive billiard cloth. Suspended ceilings require special provision for the fitting of lighting shades in exactly the required position centred over the table. A plug-in light point is required over each table so that the lighting unit can be disconnected for servicing and repainting. Each table lighting unit should be switched separately from a booking or control point. Alternatively, where there is no permanent attendant on duty in the billiard room (a situation which would normally appertain in a sports centre) a convenient way of collecting revenue is by using coin operated prepayment meters to control the table lighting. The meter(s) need to be wall-mounted, and wiring should be preferably installed during building operations. However, a meter can be added to an existing installation using a double-pole circuit.

The special-match table scoreboard should be illuminated.
● Games of billiards and snooker do not generate much noise, but the degree of concentration required to play the games properly calls for a measure of sound insulation to prevent disturbance from noise outside the playing area.

Equipment: fixtures and storage
These games require the provision of a score board approximately 900mm × 600mm × 50mm screwed to the wall, close to the table.

Storage will be required for a soft table cover and if, as usual, some cues are supplied for general use, then security considerations suggest that cues should be stored and issued at the booking point. If stored in the playing area provision should be made for one common wall-mounted cue rack, the siting of which depends on the layout of the tables. However, it should be fixed well away from any heating source.

Special considerations
Tables must not be moved once they have been set up and they must be adequately protected when not in use. A firm level floor/special-match tables need adequate space for players and elevated spectators/plug-in table lighting trough with tungsten lamps and a common illuminance (lux) for all standards of play/good ventilation.

Sources of reference and advice
The Billiards and Snooker Control Council
Billiards Trade Association Group

* Based on an example calculation given in IES *Lighting Guide: Sport*, which is otherwise superseded by this Data Sheet.

30
Box lacrosse

1 *Space diagram of enclosed playing area. Box lacrosse is played in North America and the English Lacrosse Union would like to introduce an indoor version into the UK. It is a lacrosse stick, hard floor version of ice hockey, including side barrier, 'sin-bins' and other similarities. Note the additional safety netting above the barrier, particularly high behind the goals. Note: All floor markings 50mm (2in) in width. Goals (9) 1220mm × 1220mm (4ft × 4ft) pegged 1220mm (4ft) behind the goal line. The centre zone (3) consists of two solid lines located 3350mm (11ft) on each side of the exact centre of the playing area and parallel to the end boards*

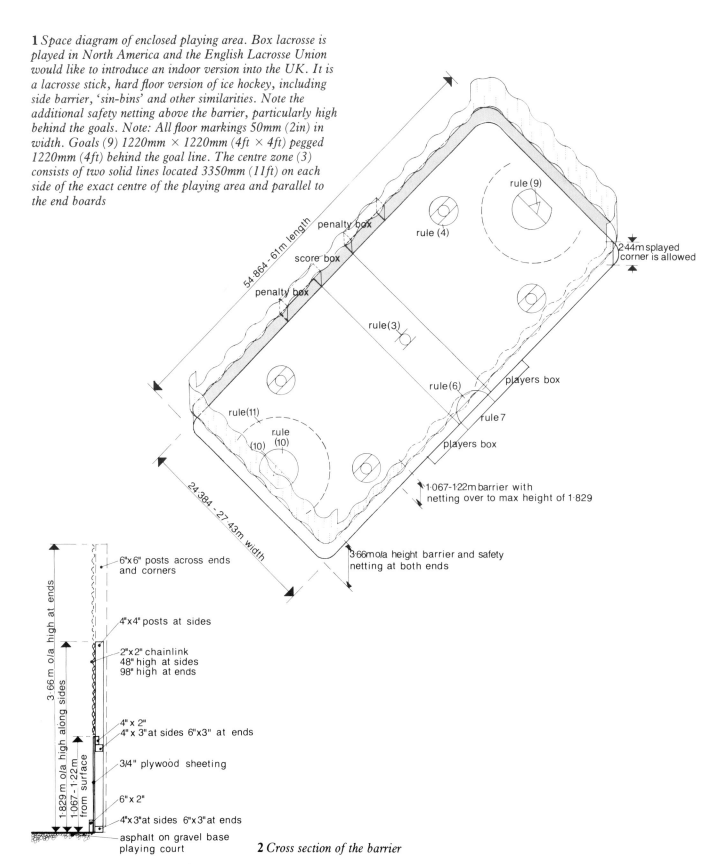

2 *Cross section of the barrier*

31
Cycle racing

1 *Skol indoor meeting, Wembley 1979. Note the bridge access to centre area for officials control, trade displays and advertising, bars and trackside hospitality boxes*

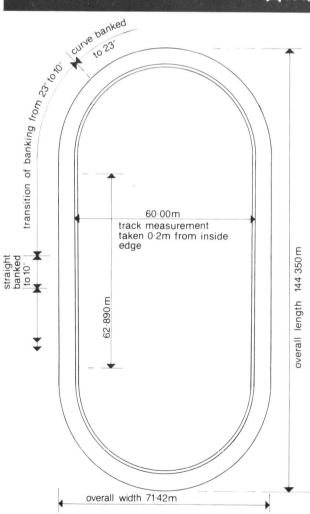

curve banked to 23°

transition of banking from 23° to 10°

60·00m
track measurement taken 0·2m from inside edge

62·890 m

straight banked to 10°

overall length 144·350 m

overall width 71·42m

33¹/3m local track

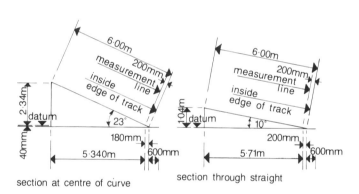

section at centre of curve

section through straight

3a *Sections through a 333⅓m track*

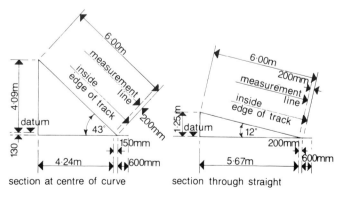

section at centre of curve

section through straight

2 *Plan of 333⅓m local cycle track. Olympic tracks are 7·0m wide. Velodromes have usually endeavoured to fit a 200m athletics track within a cycle circuit, but there is now a growing official view that the two sports are incompatible, both for essential training and competition purposes. An indoor velodrome should have a 333⅓m track and be capable of seating at least 3,000 to 4,000 spectators. This should be capable of expansion to 10,000 using temporary seating for World or European Championships*

3b *Sections through a 250m track. A demountable 200m or 250m track could be included in a brief for a multi-purpose indoor arena, but with a considerable loss of spectator capacity due to the steeply banked sides.*

32
Darts

Space requirements

When planning for darts enough space must be allowed around the board to ensure safety (see **2, 3** for critical dimensions). Avoid placing boards adjacent to a doorway. If more than one board is to be provided a side-by-side arrangement is best allowing 1·5m between throwing lanes.

Multi-purpose use of space

Darts requires to be sited away from other activities for safety reasons, but the space can be used for other purposes when the game is not being played. In view of the wall finish (see below) the space could also serve for exhibitions. See also Volume 2, Part II, Technical Study 5.

Spectator facilities

Spectators should be seated behind the throw line. They should not be seated between throw lanes in championship events because spectators' movement will distract the players. They can be seated at tables and chairs or on mobile bleacher units.

Enclosing elements and finishes

The wall surface on which a dart board is hung should be faced with a material that is not likely to be defaced by the darts while not damaging the points of the darts. A fibreboard or similar lining is therefore recommended. The floor area beneath the board also needs to be protected for the same reason, **2**.

For match play and championships it is desirable to isolate the space by means of a curtain or sliding/folding partition to ensure that players' concentration is not affected by outside noise.

Internal environment

● A background temperature of 15·6°C is desirable and adequate ventilation will be required to cope with players' bouts of concentrated smoking.

● Lighting of the board by normal and/or artificial means is essential (see **2**).

● The pitch of excitement reached over a closely fought contest is often worked off by the players when the darts have been thrown and the score totted up. Such uninhibited manifestations of joy or despair are characteristic of few other games. Conversely the concentration required in match play or championships should not be disturbed by noise from outside. A reasonable degree of insulation against transmission of sound and the provision of absorbent surfaces within the dart-playing space are therefore desirable.

1 *Photo: Kent Press Pictures*

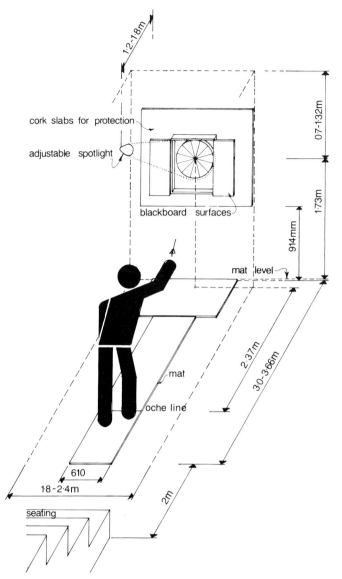

cork slabs for protection

adjustable spotlight

blackboard surfaces

mat level

mat

oche line

seating

1·2-1·8m

0·7-1·32m

1·73m

914mm

2·37m

3·0-3·66m

2m

610

1·8-2·4m

2 *Space diagram showing lighting*

Storage
The dart board, often contained within a box, is generally a fixture and needs no storage. The mat is rolled up and needs to be stored away. It measures approximately 6m long × ·3m diam when rolled up and weights about 15 kg.

Governing body and source of further reference
The main promoter of darts is the British Darts Organisation which organises the area and national championships. Further specialist advice can be obtained from it.

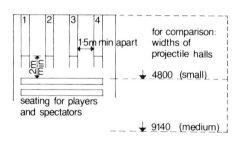

1 2 3 4

1·5m min apart

2m min

for comparison:
widths of
projectile halls

4800 (small)

seating for players
and spectators

9140 (medium)

3 *Suggested layout for darts across the width of a projectile hall*

33
Fives: Rugby fives

Handball games with softer balls are played largely in Ireland and the USA. In England the name 'fives' has been used since the 17th century at least. It is now believed to be derived from the bound or gloved five fingers, as in 'bunch of fives' meaning the fist.

The game is one of the oldest in the world. As soon as the ball was invented it was knocked against a wall or angles of walls on all sorts of improvised courts, in castle keeps and in churchyards. Rugby fives is like squash rackets differing in that it is played with the gloved hands and not a racket, in a smaller court measuring 8·53 × 5·49m. The court also requires a harder composition walls and floor because the game is played with a hard and lively ball **1, 2**.

Further source of reference
The Rugby Fives Association can supply an outline description and specification for the construction of courts.
For Eton fives see Data Sheet **57**.

1 *Photo: St Paul's School, London*

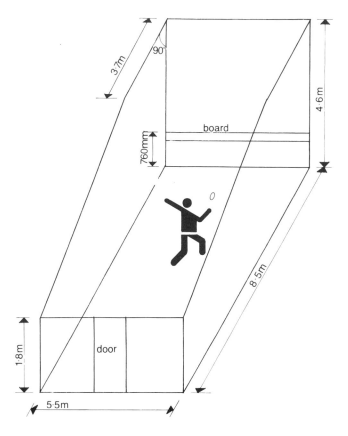

2 *A standard rugby fives court has four walls with no buttresses, and is used for both singles and doubles play*

34
Gymnastics training pits

Background
Landing pits were developed in East Europe and Russia in the late 1960s and 1970s for gymnastic training purposes. It is now recognised they have made a significant contribution to the speed with which young gymnasts can advance their skills, and this has been reflected in the competitive achievements of these countries.

The advantage of foam-filled pits is that they remove the fear of injury, particularly to the legs and ankles, on awkward landings and enable gymnasts to concentrate on their movements both on the apparatus and through the air. They also dispense with the need for instructors to catch gymnasts when they dismount from the apparatus.

Pit configuration and location
The most simple form of pit is one which enables different pieces of apparatus to be erected over it, and also serves as a landing area for tumbling and vaulting.

In multisports spaces such as sports halls pits will require covering to provide a flush finish with the surrounding sports

1 Lilleshall NSC—interior at fitting out. Photo:
Shelter-Span (UK) Limited

surface. Careful design is required to achieve a floor panel and edge protection system which can be simply and easily removed. If space is restricted it may be possible to utilise an adjoining sports area to increase the length of the run-up for vaulting and tumbling.

The most elaborate pit configuration is one which will enable each piece of apparatus to be permanently stationed over or beside the pits as has been built at Lilleshall Hall National Sports Centre.

Pit construction
It is essential to construct pits to withstand ground water pressure. This should present no problem in new work where land drains can be laid as an additional safeguard to the construction, but it is not so easy to achieve in conversion work where the construction of pits can also interfere with existing foundations.

At Lilleshall the pit walls and floor are of 250mm 30/20 reinforced concrete, ringed at low level with a land drain connected to a soakaway. It is important to provide for fixing of the edge protection and equipment sockets in the rim of the pits.

In existing halls of sufficient height, pits can be formed by raising the whole or part of the floor level as has been done in

some older East European gymnasia. The suspended floor can then be detailed as required but 'causeway' run-ups and podiums will need safeguarding with balustrades.

Pit lining
The bottom is packed to a depth of 1m with blocks of foam of a density to provide a progressive resistance to impact, and the upper 1m is filled with loose-laid strips of foam—offcuts from the upholstering industry are adequate. Effective protection of the pit edges is of the utmost importance. At Lilleshall the edge detail consists of 8lb foam in L-shaped blocks located in a continuous band around the concrete rim by a nylon reinforced pvc cover, tensioned between hard-wood battens. A method of ventilating the space beneath the foam should be provided to prevent the foam from becoming foul.

Sources of reference
For further technical details, and experience from Lilleshall, consult TUS.

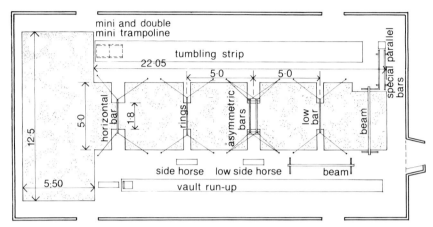

2 *Lilleshall—plan (Architects: Technical Unit for Sport)*

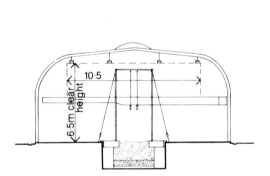

3 *Lilleshall—section*

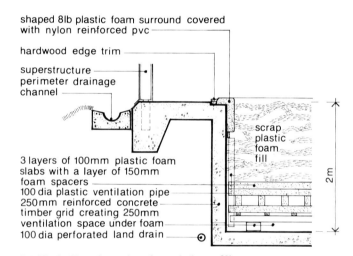

4 *Lilleshall—pit section through foam fill*

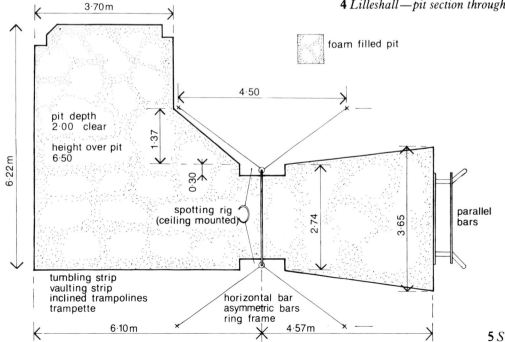

5 *Small multi-purpose pit*

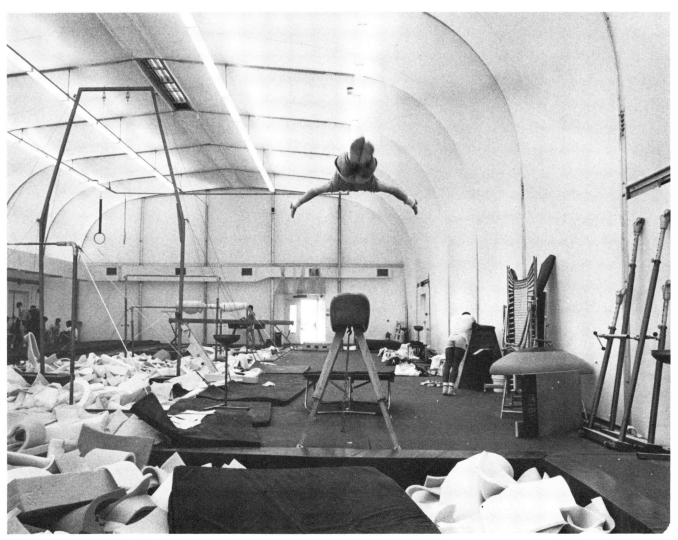

6 *Lilleshall—interior in use. Photo: David Butler*

7 *Edgetrim detail*

35
Irish handball

Introduction
In the late 1800s the traditional Irish handball court was an open-air court, varying in dimensions. Today's modern indoor court, with its ceiling, flush lighting, maple floor, glass-back wall and central heating, bears little resemblance to earlier courts and appears more like a squash or fives court. The game is also related to Spanish Pelota (see Data Sheet 36).
Court or Irish Handball is a ball game played by two players (singles) or two pairs (doubles) on a walled court. The ball is struck with a gloved hand in such a way that it is difficult for the opponent to return it. The court has four walls with the ceiling, a playing surface also. The game is identical to that played in the USA; however the YMCA's widely play a one-wall American handball, **2**.

Space requirements
An Irish Handball Association international handball court requires a total space approximately 19m long × 6·1m wide internally, with a finished floor to ceiling height of 6·1m. The playing area of the court is 12·2m × 6·1m × 6·1m high, and is generally separated from the viewing area by means of a glass back fourth wall. Similar to squash, spectators are seated on stepped benching or retractable tiers, or in a gallery underneath which can be housed the dressing and toilet facilities.
Courts to non-international dimensions have a playing area of approximately 18 × 9m with a pitched roof but these are rapidly falling out of favour.
The court for the four-wall game must conform to the measurements shown in **2**.

Floor
Flooring should consist of birdseye maple, whiterock maple, or other approved hardwood flooring, laid on 75 × 50mm ventilated battens, hilti nailed to a 150mm reinforced and damp-proofed concrete ground slab.
Flooring should be given a single light coat of proprietary sealer to avoid a slippery polished surface.

Court markings
The lines on the floor must be red and 38mm wide.

Walls
External load-bearing brick walls should consist of an 113mm outer skin, a 75mm cavity with approved insulation and an inner skin of 225mm brick or concrete block, reinforced every fourth course.
Internal dividing walls should consist of at least 225mm brickwork or blockwork, the end wall being either 225mm or 113mm thick.

Glass-back wall
This should consist of a 9·3mm Triplex plate screwed to a metal or timber frame with a 0·76m centrally-placed armour-plated glass door (similar to that in squash courts). The overall minimum height of the glass-back wall should be

1 *Glass-back court at Queen's University. Photo: Belfast Telegraph*

3·658m. The wall may require to be braced with glass fins at about 1·22m centres.
For detailed specifications consult the Irish Handball Association.

Internal wall finishes
The designer should render and float these in sand and cement and finish fine with a steel trowel. Alternatively, a squash plaster finish will give an improved surface. A vee joint should be formed vertically in the long wall immediately outside the back wall of playing area. All walls should be given three coats of white co-polymer.

Ceiling
The ceiling in standard courts is flat with recessed lighting as the ceiling is used in play. It need generally only extend over the playing area and should consist of 12mm plywood fixed to the roof joists at 450mm centres. All joints should be taped and a 3mm movement gap left between sheets.
A 10mm gap should be left along the wall perimeter. Adequate roof insulation should be laid between the trusses at ceiling level and impact-resistant lighting panels should be fixed to finish flush with the ceiling.

Internal environment

• If natural daylighting is provided, roof lights in the playing area approximate to 20 per cent of the floor area of the playing court, should finish flush with the ceiling, and should be drilled to prevent condensation forming.

• Lighting provision should consist of 10 twin 2400mm-long fluorescent lights in the playing area, parallel to the front wall, with 5 on each side of the court.

These may be wired to slot meters if required. The lighting levels required are similar to those for squash, ie 150 lux at floor level for recreational use; 300 lux for club and county competitions and 500 lux for national and international standards.

• The system should provide four air changes per hour.

• When planning heating, two no 3-kilowatt fan heaters are normally considered sufficient to provide background heating to both the court and the viewing stand. These should be swivel-mounted on the side walls of the court, immediately behind the glass-back wall.

Critical factors

In all types of court construction the following basic principles must be adhered to:

• A high standard of plastering within the playing area

• A good quality hardwood floor

• A flush ceiling

• Sufficient background heating to enable court temperatures to be maintained at approximately 13°C

• Approximately 20 per cent natural daylighting to enable the courts to be used at minimum cost by young people

• Artificial lighting to be controlled by coin meters in order to obtain revenue

• A glass-back wall in all courts with some major viewing areas

• In larger centres, discussion should be held prior to court design, with various television companies, in order to incorporate facilities inside the courts to enable a game to be televised.

Sources of reference

Sports Council of Northern Ireland
General advice on court construction can at all times be obtained from the Officers of the Irish Handball Council, Croke Park, Dublin 3, who publish a more detailed specification, *Handball court construction*

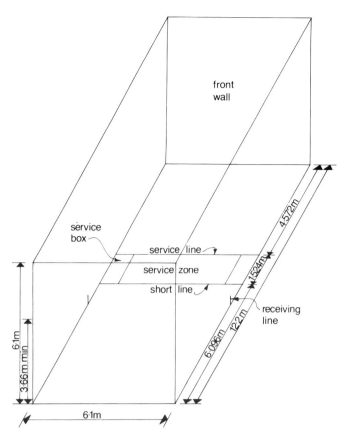

3 *Space diagram of the international size court which is smaller than the earlier traditional court*

2 *American Handball Court, Central YMCA, London*

36
Pelota

Pelota is a fast ball game played in a three-walled court (fronton) by two players, or by several teams of players. Players attempt to hit a ball (pelota) with a wicket basket (cesta) against the front wall (frontis) so that their opponents will be unable to return it and will therefore lose a point. The game originated in northern Spain. The rules given here are for the game now played in the United States.

The court
The court has three walls, **1**. The front wall is called the frontis, the back wall the rebote, and the side wall the lateral. The frontis is made of granite blocks while the rebote, lateral, and floor are made of gunite, a pressurized cement.
The fourth side of the court has a clear screen through which spectators watch the game. To comply with UK safety factors this would need to consist of shatter-proof and possibly fire-proof glazing.
The court is divided into fifteen numbered areas. The serving zone is the space between areas 4 and 7.

Source of reference
Rules of the Game, Diagram Visual Information Ltd

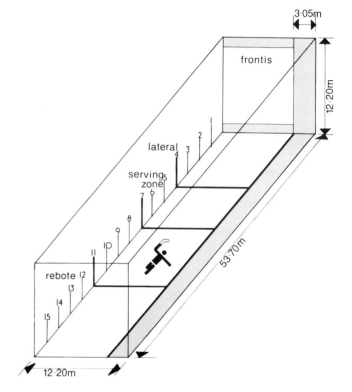

1 *Space diagram*

37
Rackets

This is another racket-and-ball game played in England, the USA and Canada, **1**. Two or four players participate in a court enclosed by four walls, giving a floor area generally of 18·3m × 9·1m (60ft × 30ft). The surrounding walls are 9·1m (30ft) high and the service line on the front walls is 2·9m (9ft 6in) from the floor. The back wall is 4·12m (13ft 6in) high, **2**. The lay-out of the court is similar to that of its modern and more widely popular offshoot, squash rackets, but the dimensions are larger. The floor is of stone or asphalt and the ball is solid-cored.

The front or main wall, facing the players as they enter the court, is traversed by two horizontal lines: the higher or service line, or 'cut' line. The service must be struck above this. The play line, near floor-level and formed by a board fastened to the wall, determines the lower limit on the front wall to which all returns must be directed.

Sources of reference
Tennis and Rackets Association

1 *Photo: Peter J. Smith and Stanley Paul and Co. Ltd*

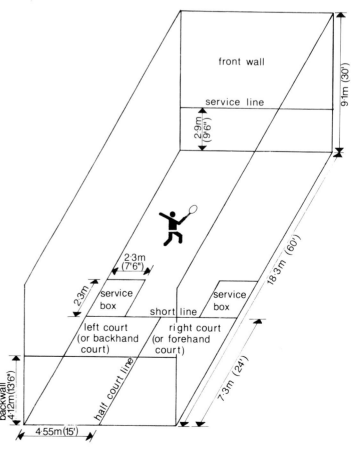

2 *Space diagram*

38
Racquetball

The first major racquetball championships were held in the United States in 1969. Racquetball was first played in Britain during the summer of 1975, but did not start to spread until early 1976 when equipment first became available. Similar to squash, and sharing its court, racquetball can be played by anyone with a little stamina and an eye for a ball. There is little advantage through strength, so women can compete on equal terms with men, and older players with younger enthusiasts.

Designed to stimulate the use of squash facilities during 'off-peak periods', the housewife will enjoy the advantage of playing during the day when courts are less heavily booked. The popularity in Britain of racquet games in general, and the initial enthusiastic reaction to racquetball in particular, suggests this new game will continue its growth trend in Britain. It is now being played at some 25 to 300 leisure centres, squash clubs and schools.

Siting
In the UK, racquetball is played on squash* and Irish handball courts and is complementary to squash rather than rivalling it. It is played with a specially designed racquet which looks very much like a miniature tennis racquet, **1**. The ball is twice the diameter of a squash ball and has much more bounce. Unlike a squash ball it does not need warming up and it is non-marking.

The rules are similar to those for squash, the principal difference being the rules for service, which requires that the ball should be bounced before being served.

Racquetball in the USA is played in a court 12·19 × 6·096m (40 × 20ft) as opposed to the British squash court which is 9·754 × 6·4m. The racquetball court in the USA does not have a board (or tin, as it is commonly called.)

Court markings
All the court markings for squash apply except that the Cut Line (the line across the front wall in a squash court) is ignored.

Source of reference
British Racquetball Association with the National Squash Federation

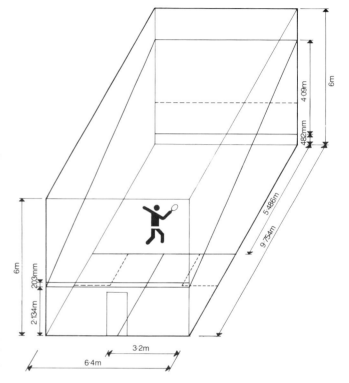

1 *Racquetball in a squash court*

---

* For squash court dimensions see Volume 2, Part II.

39
Real tennis

Dimensions
The dimensions of real tennis courts are not precisely uniform, but the playing area at floor level is approximately 29·3m long × 9·8m wide (96ft × 32ft). Above the penthouses it becomes 33·5m × 11·9m (110 ft × 39 ft). The roof is about 9m (30 ft) above the floor. Sometimes it contains glass so that the court is naturally top lit, **3**.

Floors
The floors of courts are made of stone or concrete composition. The most favoured stones are limestone and Caen stone; the cement is Portland cement or Bickley's patent non-sweating composition. Walls are of stone or brick coated with the same cement or composition. Floors are normally black or red, walls black or slate-grey. Lamp-black diluted with bullock's blood and ox-galls is the traditional receipe for blackening floors and walls: but 20th-century redecorations mostly have to rely on synthetic stone paint and matt emulsion.

Sources of reference
Tennis and Rackets Association
Real Tennis in Scotland: Article in *Scotsquash*, December 1977

2 *Real tennis at Hampton Court*

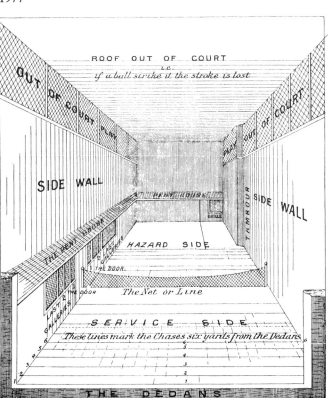

1 *Hampton Court. The original 16th-century English indoor sports hall for the ancient original tennis—or real tennis—c. 1400, from which developed the outdoor lawn game. With acknowledgements to the Tennis and Rackets Association and the early Royal Courts of France*

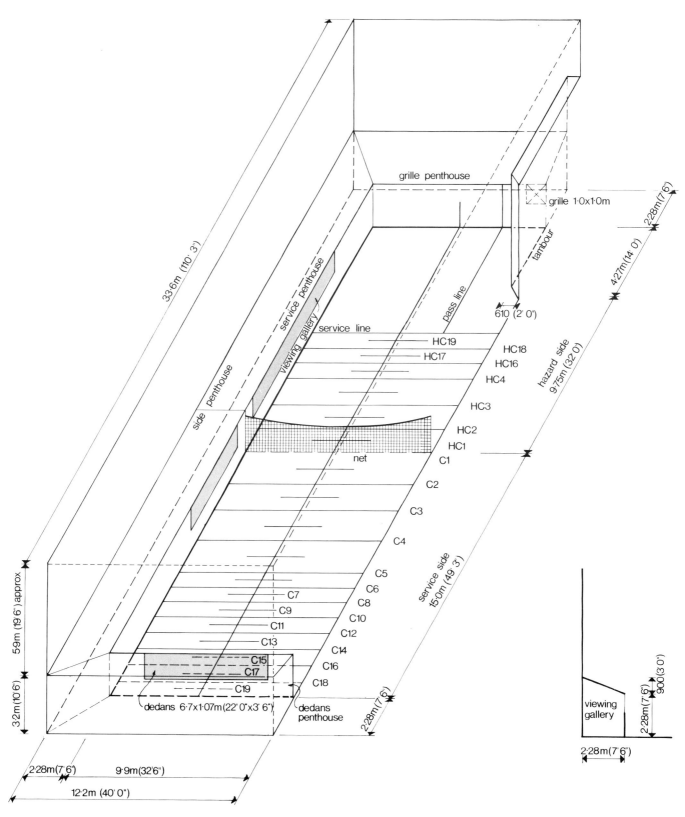

grille penthouse

grille 1·0x1·0m

tambour

33·6m (110' 3')

service penthouse

viewing gallery

side penthouse

service line

pass line

610 (2' 0")

2·28m(7'6')

4·27m(14' 0')

hazard side 9·75m (32' 0')

HC19
HC17
HC18
HC16
HC4
HC3
HC2
HC1

net

C1
C2
C3
C4
C5
C6
C7
C8
C9
C10
C11
C12
C13
C14
C15
C16
C17
C18
C19

service side 15·0m (49' 3')

5·9m (19' 6") approx

3·2m(10'6')

dedans 6·7x1·07m (22' 0"x3' 6")

dedans penthouse

2·28m(7'6')

2·28m(7'6')
9·9m(32'6")
12·2m (40' 0")

viewing gallery

2·28m(7'6')

9·00(3'0')

2·28m(7'6')

3 *Approximate dimensions of the court at Hampton Court Palace, reputed to be the widest, and one of the longest known. Numbered lines on the service side of the net have the following conventional designations: C1 chase the line, C2 chase first gallery, C3 chase the door, C4 chase second gallery, C5 chase a yard worse than last gallery, C6 chase last gallery, C7 chase half a yard worse than six, C8 chase six, C9 chase five and six, C10 chase five, C11 chase four and five, C12 chase four, C13 chase three and four, C14 chase three, C15 chase two and three, C16 chase two, C17 chase one and two, C18 chase one yard, C19 chase half a yard. Lines are numbered correspondingly on the hazard side. HC Hazard chase*

4 *Section through side and ends—the original penthouse*

40
Riding and indoor equestrianism

Basic requirements for a riding centre
The following have been extracted from British Horse Society requirements:
Instructional
- A covered riding school (**1–4**)
- An outdoor manege (see p 124)
- A show jumping arena
- Cross-country fences

Administrative
- Stables (**5**)
- Saddle or tack room (**6**)
- Forage store (**7**)
- General storage
- Manager's office
- Lavatories and washing facilities
- Club room
- Canteen
- Living accommodation
- Car and horse box park (for loading space see p 125)

A covered riding school
To provide an all-weather area for riding it will be found that covered facilities of some sort are essential.
Covered schools are of many different standards. The BHS's National Equestrian Centre, **1**, consists of a riding area 61 × 24·4m—large enough to contain an international-size arena

2 Junior jumping at Ivory Equestrian Centre, Hertfordshire. Photo: MVR Photographic

and in which to hold dressage and show jumping events. Seating for 300 has been provided along one side. At the other end of the scale it is possible to provide a suitable area under a Dutch barn, of which the sides are only clad for 3m from the eaves and wattle hurdles enclose the floor.

1 National Equestrain Centre, Stoneleigh. Note the excessive solar top light and surrounding kicking boards. Photo: Monty, Birmingham

Whatever the standard of the building it is essential that the indoor riding space should be at least 24 × 44m, which is just the minimum size required for an ordinary dressage arena, and equestrian centre indoor show jumping, **2**. The full size space is 64 × 24m, as shown in **3**. Both sizes include a space of 2m which must be left all round the riding area.

All-weather riding floor surface
The floor of the school is of great importance. Provided the surface of the ground is hard, flat and well drained, a covering of 50mm or 75mm fine sand well rolled in, mixed with commercial salt, to which 25mm of wood shavings may be added from time to time, provides an excellent working surface. Care should be taken to ensure that the covering is not too deep at the start. It is easier to add material than to take it out. The surface should be first rolled or ridden in. Unless watering facilities are easily available, the use of salt will avoid dust. Wood fibre specialist surfaces are also available.

Kicking boards
These are a basic functional requirement around all sides. A light coloured finish best reflects most natural top light and provides a useful contrasting background for an instructor to observe more easily the horse's leg movements, and riders' aids, particularly during transitions. The minimum height is normally 1·8m and the boards are inclined outwards at about 100° with the floor. In front of spectators, kicking boards are reduced to height of 914mm.

Source of reference
Further detailed advice can be obtained from the British Horse Society and the British Show Jumping Association. Refer also to 'Construction of Covered Schools', in *Stable Management* August/September 1979, and the Building Study in the *Architects' Journal*, 28 November 1973.

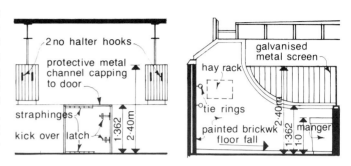

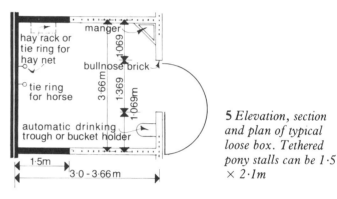

5 *Elevation, section and plan of typical loose box. Tethered pony stalls can be 1·5 × 2·1m*

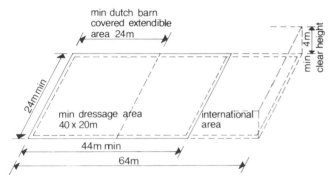

3 *Riding school and jumping areas. The broken line indicates the clear area inside the kicking boards. The BSJA preferred arena size is about 49–52m × 24–26m. The FEI rules for indoor international CSIO and CSI events require that 'the area of the arena must be as near as possible a minimum of 2500 square metres'. Practice jump and collecting areas and a control/judges box are also required*

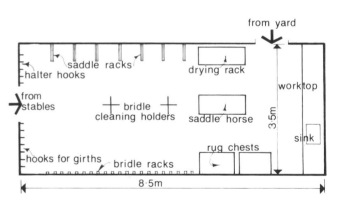

6 *Tack room plan and details*

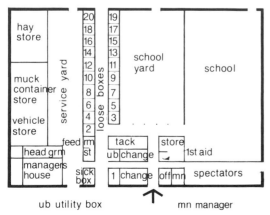

4 *Plan of Lea Bridge Riding School (Architects: Lee Valley Region Park Authority)*

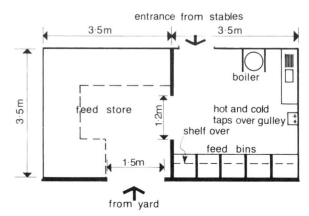

7 *Plan of feed store*

41
Roller hockey, skating and artistic skating

The National Skating Association (NSA) writes that roller sports roughly fall into two categories:
- Recreational skating—public skating, **1**.
- Skilled skating—which divides into the following disciplines:

1. Artistic skating—figures and dance, **2**.
2. Speed skating—rink and track (see also outdoor skating, p 127).
3. Roller hockey—which has its own governing body, the National Roller Hockey Association of Great Britain, **3**.

There is also roller disco dancing which is really an entertainment rather than a sport.

Roller sports impose critical problems, for example:
- need for specially hard resistant floor, **4**, and sealants, and programmed maintenance. It is essential to note that skateboarding and roller skating indoors can generate dust where smooth concrete or existing composition block floors are used unless an extremely durable seal is applied. Manufacturers should be consulted before floors are subjected to either skateboarding or roller skating.
- need to eliminate grit: walls may need to be sealed
- additional storage space
- spectator space: particularly for casual viewing
- roller hockey requires rounded corners within square cornered spaces
- strengthened skirtings and additional buffer and grip rails are needed.

Like many pastimes roller skating has developed and it must be noted that new techniques and equipment are now being used and future builders of rinks should fully understand the problems and possibilities associated with this activity. Readers should consult the governing bodies, who with TUS are preparing a Data Sheet to give updated facilities and techniques requirements for these sports.

2 Artistic roller skating. Photo: Sports Council Publications

1 Recreational skating at Buckmore Park sports hall, Chatham, Kent. Photo: Fred Dean

3 Roller hockey in Pier Pavilion Leisure Centre, Herne Bay, Kent. For hockey dimensions see the space diagram on p 126. Photo: Fred Dean

4 *Flooring patterns and details. The National Skating Association recommend that the floor should be of maple or similar hard wood strips 50mm wide and preferably not more than 65mm wide, to run the long way of the floor and to be as long as possible. At the ends of the rink the strips should turn with the run of the skater. The strip-floor should be laid on a sub-floor of soft wood set in pitch or a similar mastic on a flat concrete floor. The result is a floor without a cavity to become an echo chamber. After surfacing by machining, the whole floor is coated two or three times with a very dense polyurethane type of compound. Noise and dust are eliminated. Nylon and plastic wheels replace wooden wheels, and provide perfectly quiet skating*

a *The log-cabin floor shown is least expensive. It offers all the advantages of durable, smooth maple with a simple board pattern to lower the cost of installation*

b *The fan-type floor pattern is more complex, with the floor grain pattern following the flow of rink traffic more closely*

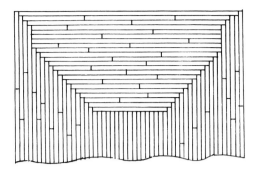

a

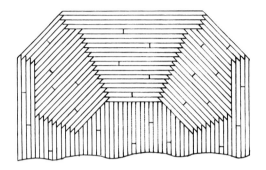

b

42
Rowing training

Siting
Rowing training requires a specially constructed tank as shown in **1** and **2**.

Floor
Flooring should be laid to fall and with a non-slip finish.

Surrounding surfaces or enclosure
This should be non-corrosive and impervious.

Internal environment
• Background heating to a level 10–13°C is desirable. There are no special requirements for ventilation or lighting.
• Noise control will be needed if most surfaces are hard.

Storage
No special storage facilities are required.

Special requirements
Drainage to empty to clean out periodically.

Source of reference
Amateur Rowing Association

1 *Rowing tank at Elmbridge Leisure Centre, Walton on Thames. Photo: Derek Evans*

2 *Plan and section AA*

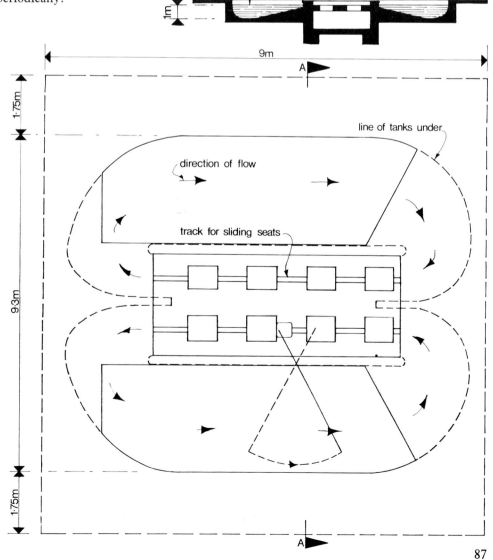

43
Tenpin bowling

Space planning

The overall space requirements for this game are shown in **2**. Space behind the lanes must be provided for the storage of pins, pinspotters spare parts and maintenance supplies. There also should be a mechanic's workshop or workbench. Ideally, there should be one large or two small rooms in the rear of the building for these purposes. If such rooms are not available, the servicing aisle behind the pinspotters should be at least 1·8m wide; otherwise ·91m would be wide enough. If the bowling pin maintenance is located behind the machines, then an approved extractor fan and vent should be provided to remove fumes and dust.

The overall length of a bowling lane (including the approach area, the lane itself, and the automatic pinspotter) is 25m to 25·5m depending upon the type of pinspotter.

Bowler's settee area

This area should be 3·0m to 3·2m in depth and should be raised ·33m above the concrete floor-level of the lanes area. It should be covered with vinyl tiles or equally suitable material.

Spectator lounge area

Rather than spectator seats behind the lanes, tables and chairs are recommended where space permits. Waitress service may be maintained between the bar, snack bar and this

1 *Photo: The Central Council of Physical Recreation*

area. This area, which is actually part of the concourse, should be at least ·15m higher than the bowlers' area and could be carpeted.

Bowlers' coat racks

Closet space for outer garments is recommended behind the bowlers' settees.

Concourse

The concourse area should be wide enough to provide easy access from the bowlers' area to the other facilities. It is suggested that approximately 4·5m be left free between the tables behind the lanes and the toilets, lockers and other facilities. The entire concourse area could be carpeted.

Control counter

The control counter should be raised and so located that the lanes and entrances can be observed at all times. Shoe rentals and special checking facilities should be part of the control counter. It is recommended that part of the counter itself should be glass show-windows for the display of merchandise and promotional materials.

Manager's office

A small room, preferably connected to the control counter, should be provided to enable the manager to carry out his office duties in connection with the general administration of the bowling centre.

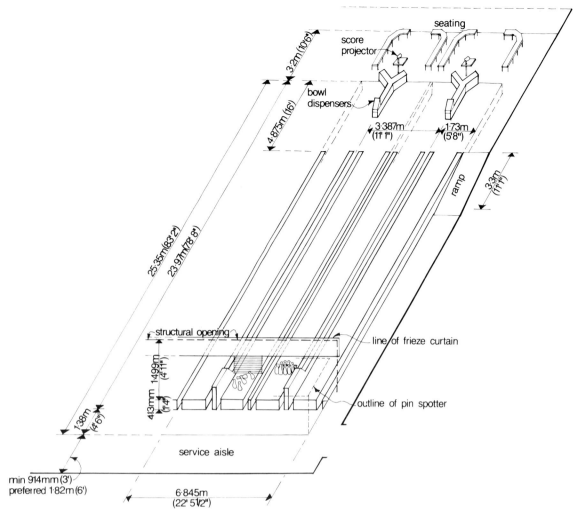

2 *Space diagram of bowling area*

Bowling lane dimensions	
No.	Width in metres
2	3·46
4	6·85
6	10·23
8	13·62
10	17·01
12	20·40
14	23·78
16	27·17
18	30·56
20	33·95
22	37·33
24	40·72

Note: The above dimensions do not allow space for an access aisle (minimum width 0·76m) leading from the concourse area to the machines

Toilets
The number of fixtures and facilities is governed usually by local government regulations. The facilities are roughly calculated on a basis of 5 persons per lane with allowances for spectator and snack bar seating. Toilet rooms should be located where they are easily accessible to the bowlers and near the lockers and changing rooms.

Lockers
Lockers should be provided for rental to regular bowlers to store their equipment. It is suggested that 10 lockers be provided for each pair of lanes.

Snack bar
There should be a snack counter as a service to the bowlers, but a large food operation is not recommended except in instances where the area is large enough to support a restaurant.

Bar and cocktail lounge
A bar and cocktail lounge may be included if space allows and if local laws permit.

All-purpose room
At least one all-purpose room should be included in the building plan. This would serve as a meeting room for leagues and clubs and could be used as a nursery during the day. It could also serve as a changing room for tournaments and special events.

Other ancillary spaces
Plans should provide also for a cleaners' room, storage rooms, heating plant or air-conditioning room, telephones and a public address system etc.

Location of the building
The building should be located on a site or in a property with expansion potential. It should be easily accessible to main traffic arteries with ample parking facilities and entrances adjacent to parking areas. If possible canopies should be provided over entrances.

Source of reference and further advice
British Tenpin Bowling Association

44
Weight training

Siting

Any hall designed for strength training should include facilities for both weight-lifting and weight training. It is vitally important that an area be designated for heavy weight-lifting and weight training which is outside the scope of the multi-station machines. Weight lifting* is an important Olympic sport and all sports centres should ensure that facilities exist for it. The BAWLA feel it is regretable that the introduction of multi-station machines, **1**, whilst excellent for general weight training, and fitness training, have frequently completely taken up the usually limited space provided.

In addition, provision for heavy weight-training for those athletes involved in heavy field athletics is not properly catered for. The dynamics of lifting weights is lost on machines and many specialist exercises cannot be performed using them. The provision of comprehensive weight training equipment is essential, **2–4**. See also Volume 2, Part II, Technical Study 5.

The facility should in no way be shared with another sport. Weight-lifting apparatus and machines should be permanently sited and the facility should be used exclusively for that purpose. It should be supervised by staff qualified to BAWLA standards in the basics of weight-lifting and weight training, so that a facility can be used effectively for all standards of user.

Floor

In flooring a level and reasonably resilient surface is required. Rooms set aside for weight training are becoming more common in sports centres and in some cases they house a 'multi-gym', a fairly compact device offering a variety of exercises with the weights contained within or on the structure. However, where the traditional system of loose weights is retained, it is essential that besides being non-slip, the floor should be capable of resisting indentation from dropped weights and of spreading the impact on the substrate by acting as a cushion. Use of solid inflexible substrate could lead to a failure of the flooring system. Older installations of wood block have now generally been superseded by artificial materials such as battleship lino laid on asphalt and modern synthetic surfaces.

Surrounding surfaces

At least one wall must be strong enough to support equipment such as pulling machines and weight storage racks, **1–4**.

Internal environment

- Background heating of 10–13°C is desirable
- Good ventilation is essential
- Lighting is not critical
- Although noise control is not critical within the training room itself, the area should be insulated from other parts of the Centre.

* For separate facilities for weight lifting contests see Data Sheet **25** on p 50.

1 *Fitness room, Cramlington Leisure Centre. Photo: Jo Reid*

Storage

After use weights should be stored clear of the floor area either in racks or in a storage room. This is a safety and security precaution as much as for tidyness.

Basic equipment

- Lifting platform 4 × 4m
- International 200kg set of weights

NB (Both the above are essential for weight-lifting training and for competition).

- Comprehensive selection of weights and barbells
- Comprehensive selection of weights and dumbells
- Multi-station weight training machine
- Squat stands
- Benches

A wider variety of multi-station machines and systems are coming on to the market. Also water or sand filled hollow-moulded high density polyethylene sets of weights, barbells and dumbells on steel rods have been developed. It is too early to judge what impact these will have on the planning and the wear and tear of training rooms.

Source of reference and advice

For further information on facilities or equipment, specialist knowledge is available from the British Amateur Weight-lifters Association, and its publication, *Weight training facilities*.

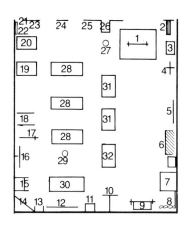

1 *Weight lifting platform and international bar*
2 *Wall bar and abdominal board*
3 *Leg and back dynamiometer*
4 *Stand with 8 bars for ladies*
5 *Leg press machine*
6 *Store cupboard*
7 *Reception table and chair*
8 *Step up bench*
9 *Barbell and dumbell rack*
10 *Pulley*
11 *Scales*
12 *Vertical storage of dumbells*
13 *Dumbell racks*
14 *Chinning bars*

15 *Calf machine*
16 *Pulley*
17 *Bicycle*
18 *Dipping bars*
19 *Safety leg machine*
20 *Leg extension and curl machine*
21 *Emergency doors*
22 *Jump test board over door*
23 *Dumbell disc trolley*
24 *Barbell racks (3)*
25 *Abdominal boards and wall bars which swing out when necessary*
26 *Vibros (2)*
27 *Slim disc (twister)*
28 *Adjustable and flat benches*
29 *Squat racks*
30 *Floor exercise mat*
31 *Two types of safety chest machines*
32 *Combination (leg and chest) machine*

2 *A fully equipped weight room at Bellahouston Sports Centre.*
Layout: BA WLA

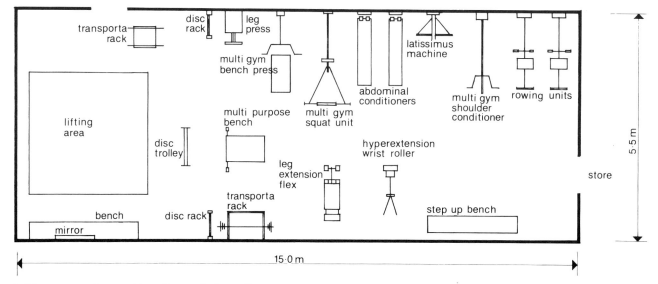

3 *Fitness room layout, Cramlington Leisure Centre*

4 *Conditioning and weight training rooms, Bunyan Recreation Centre, Bedford*

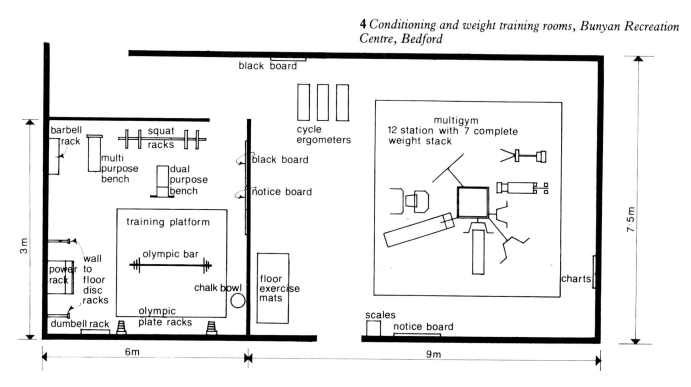

Part III Outdoor activities

45
Target and
clout archery

1 *Archery is amongst the many outdoor sports played by the disabled. Photo: David Butler*

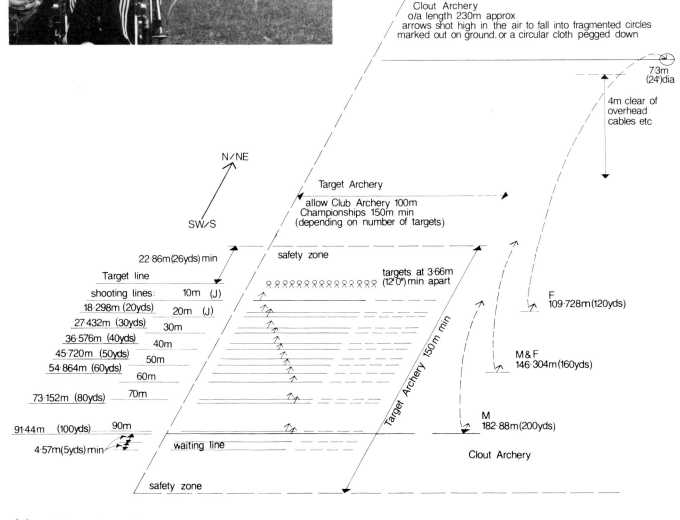

2 *Space diagram. The various distances being shot are clearly defined on the grass by white lines, tapes or spots. Archers move up and back to the 'round' being shot, and the waiting line moves accordingly. When the International Round is shot the archers remain on the original shooting line and at the change of distance the targets are moved forward (see Data Sheet **1**)*

Clout Archery
o/a length 230m approx
arrows shot high in the air to fall into fragmented circles
marked out on ground, or a circular cloth pegged down

7·3m
(24')dia

4m clear of
overhead
cables etc

N/NE

SW/S

Target Archery
allow Club Archery 100m
Championships 150m min
(depending on number of targets)

22·86m (26yds) min

safety zone

Target line

shooting lines: 10m (J)

18·298m (20yds)   20m (J)

27·432m (30yds)   30m

36·576m (40yds)   40m

45·720m (50yds)   50m

54·864m (60yds)   60m

73·152m (80yds)   70m

91·44m (100yds)   90m

4·57m(5yds) min

waiting line

safety zone

targets at 3·66m
(12'0") min apart

Target Archery 150 m min

F
109·728m (120yds)

M & F
146·304m (160yds)

M
182·88m (200yds)

Clout Archery

(J) = junior archers only

↑ = the various distances being shot are clearly defined on the grass by white lines, tapes or spots. Archers move up & back
to the 'round' being shot, & the waiting line moves accordingly

46
Athletics: track and field

1 *A Mary Peters shot. Photo: Tony Duffy*

2 *Layout guide for 400 metre running track and field events:*
(a) The number of lanes varies from six to eight depending on the type of surface and category of track facility. Lanes must be at least 1·22m wide up to a maximum of 1·25m
(b) Eight lane straights should be increased to ten or twelve lanes for training and competition intensive use. Provision of both 'home' and 'back' straights (of equal lanes) enables some simultaneous events and the direction of running can be changed to suit wind conditions
(c) Steeplechase and water jump
(d) Pole vault
(e) Long and triple jumps
(f) High jump
(g) Javelin
(h) Hammer and discus
(i) Putting the shot
(j) Paved areas.

For essential details of planning, management, site selection, events layout, detailed dimensions for field events and steeplechase, types of surfaces, track construction and maintenance, athletics training areas, equipment and storage, refer to Facilities for Athletics (track & field), *The National Playing Fields Association and The Amateur Athletic Association, Second (completely new) Edition 1980*

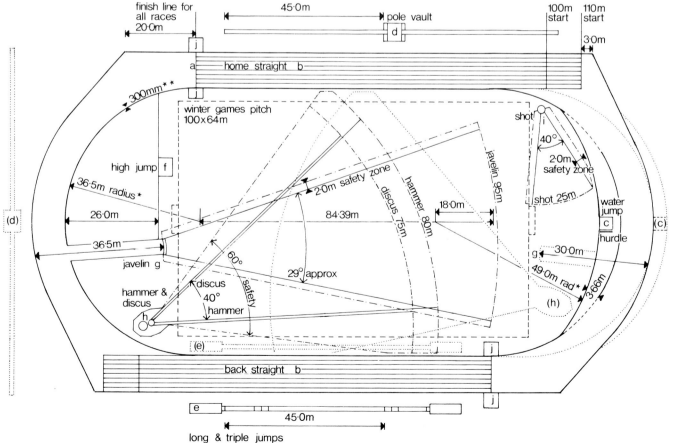

*dimension to inner face of kerb
**length of track 400m on a line 300mm from inner kerb

47
Baseball

1 *Space diagram of full-size diamond for baseball*

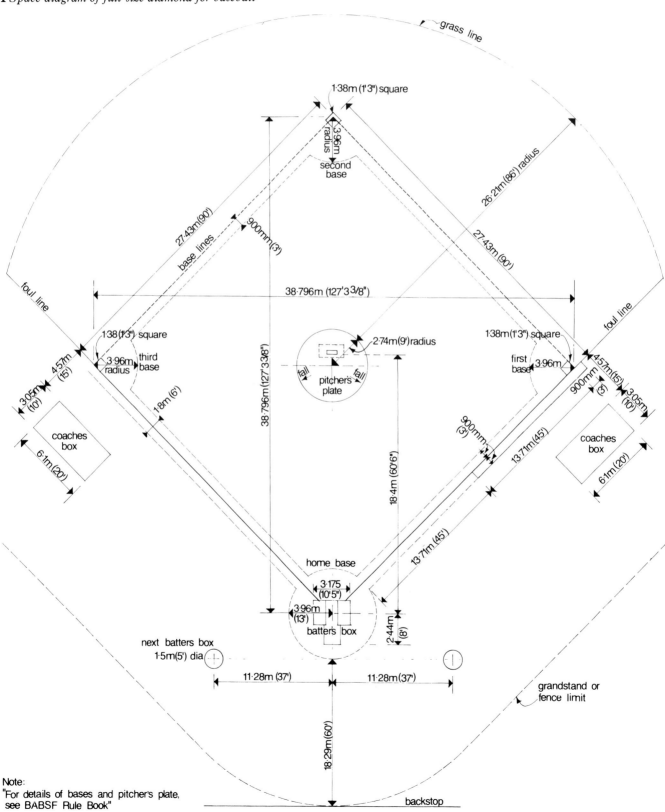

Note:
"For details of bases and pitcher's plate,
see BABSF Rule Book"

48
Bicycle polo

1 *Bicycle polo is a form of polo adapted to the use of bicycles instead of ponies; it is a team game in which the players' object is to score goals by driving a ball upfield, with the long-handled mallet carried by each players, to score between the goal posts. Photo: Home Counties Newspapers Ltd*

2 *Space diagram of bicycle polo pitch. The European version of the game—played mainly in Britain, Ireland, Belgium and France—freely modifies the basic rules of polo; a smaller grass pitch is used, and the teams (of both men and women) number six, (one of whom is a reserve), rather than four*

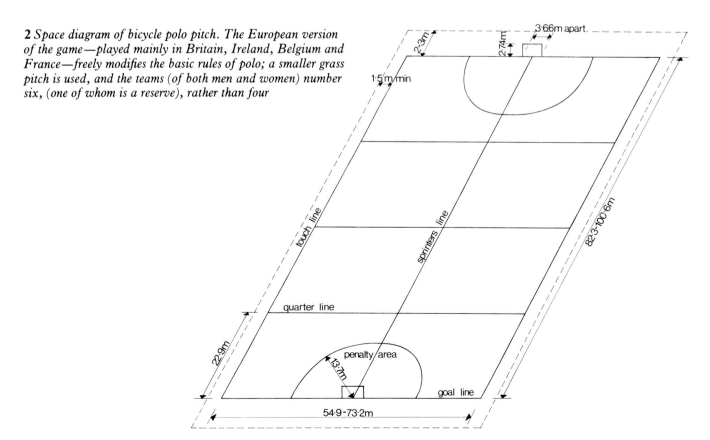

49
Bowls: lawn bowls

2 Photo: Colorsport

width

ditch 203-381mm wide and
50-200mm below green level
in depth

1 Bowling green. The flat rink green should form a square, width 36·580m minimum, 40·234m maximum. A rink width is 5·486m minimum and 5·790m maximum. The minimum distance from the outside rink to the ditch is 610mm. The maximum height of the ditch bank is 230mm and the angle not more than 35° from the perpendicular. An upright bank is recommended. Construction details are available from the NPFA

50
Camogie

1 *Ireland's native field sport for girls is a twelve-a-side stick-and-ball game based on the ancient Irish sport of hurling but modified to suit girls. Camogie is the most popular participant girls' sport in Ireland and is organised at all levels of education. County and provincial championships, and all-Ireland championships are established for club and county teams. The crooked broad-bladed stick is made from ash, and the ball or sliothar is leather covered. Photo: Sports Council for Northern Ireland*

2 *Space diagram of a camogie pitch. A distinctive feature of camogie was, until recently, a second crossbar across the top of the goal posts, but it should be noted that this requirement officially disappeared during 1979. A point is scored when the ball passes between the crossbars in the upper scoring space. A ball driven under the crossbar counts as a goal and equals 3 points. For further information and advice contact The Camogie Association and the Sports Council for Northern Ireland*

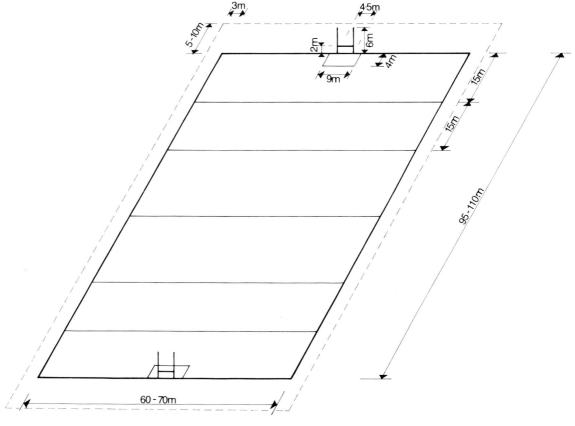

51
Cricket

3 *Photo: Photocall Features*

Cricket only

	Width A	Width 1	Length	Approx area
Seniors with	27·44m	125m	119m	1·5ha
46m boundary	18·29m	116m	119m	1·4ha
Juniors with	27·44m	107m	99m	1·1ha
37m boundary	18·29m	98m	99m	1ha

Cricket and winter games

Cricket square	Senior football	Junior football or hockey	Width 2	Length	Approx area
27·44 × 27·44m	100 × 64m	90 × 55m	164m	118m	2ha
27·44 × 18·29m	96 × 60m	82 × 46m	142m	114m	1·6ha

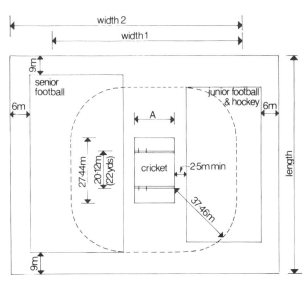

1 *Cricket field and winter games pitches*

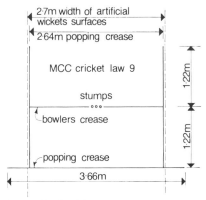

2 *Detail of cricket crease*

52
Croquet

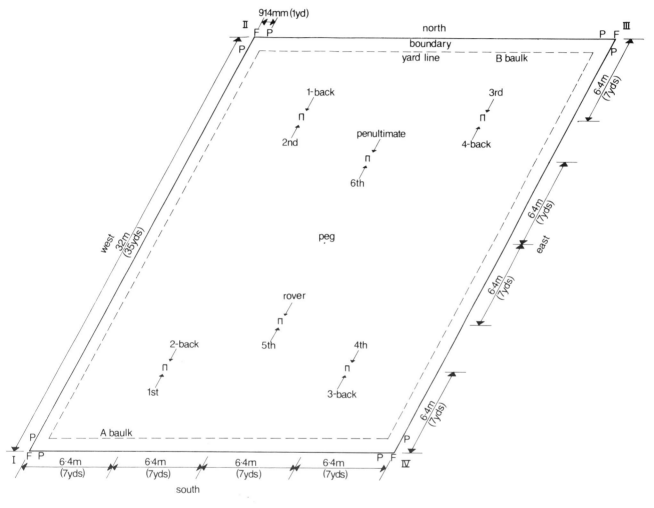

1 *Association croquet is a lawn game played with balls and a mallet on a court. Standard croquet court and setting. (P) corner pegs, (F) corner flags. The Willis setting now in use was introduced in 1922*

53
Crown green bowling

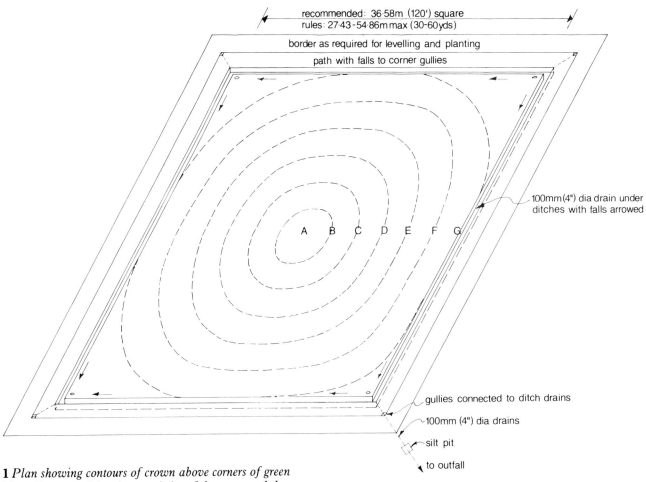

recommended: 36·58m (120') square
rules: 27·43 - 54·86m max (30-60yds)

border as required for levelling and planting

path with falls to corner gullies

A B C D E F G

100mm (4") dia drain under
ditches with falls arrowed

gullies connected to ditch drains

100mm (4") dia drains

silt pit

to outfall

1 *Plan showing contours of crown above corners of green*
*Note: Because of the characteristics of the game and the
acceptable variations between greens, the British Crown Green
Bowling Association are considering the inclusion of a
recommendation in their 1981 Handbook that for new green
construction the height of the crown be increased to 305mm
(12") on a 36·58 × 36·58m (40 × 40yd) green, and pro rata
on greens of other sizes. Construction details can be obtained
from the NPFA*

Details of camber formation

Circle radii	circle heights
A — —	254mm (10in)
B 3·05m (10ft)	248mm (9¾in)
C 6·10m (20ft)	235mm (9¼in)
D 9·14m (30ft)	216mm (8½in)
E 12·19m (40ft)	190mm (7½in)
F 15·24m (50ft)	165mm (6½in)
G 18·29m (60ft)	127mm (5in)

54
Curling

1 *Photo: Scottish Sports Council*

2 *Curling rink. Inner circles and centre lines, shown in fine line, are optional. Full details are obtainable from the Scottish Sports Council*

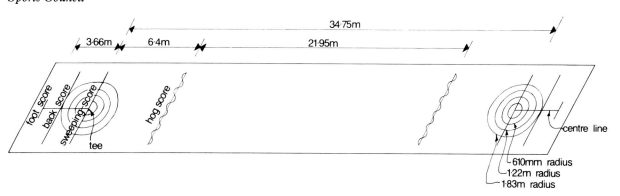

55
Cycle racing

1 *On the bank at Meadowbank Sports Centre. The current English national centre is at Leicester where the Sports Council recently contributed to the installation of a $333\frac{1}{3}$ metre international standard wooden track in the existing stadium at Saffron Lane. Ideally, outdoor tracks should also be provided with a canopy, as an alternative to the provision of an indoor velodrome. The British Cycling Federation also publishes a guide to the provision of facilities for cycle racing. Photo: City of Edinburgh*

2 *Space diagram of 333·33m circuit*

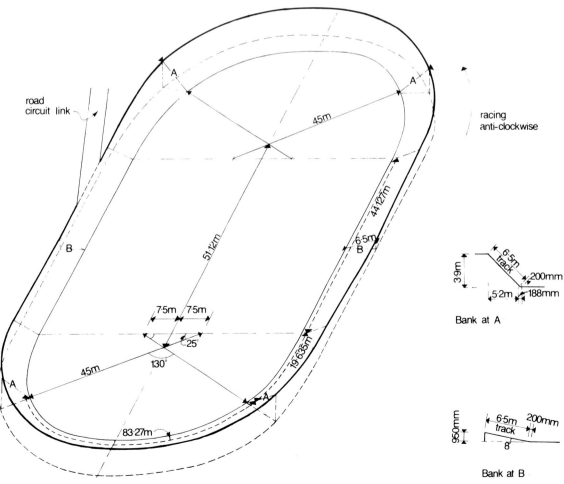

road circuit link

racing anti-clockwise

45m

44·127m

51·12m

6·5m
B

7·5m 7·5m

25°

130°

19·635m

45m

83·27m

Bank at A

6·5m track
3·9m
200mm
5·2m 188mm

Bank at B

950mm
6·5m track
200mm
8

56
Cycle speedway

1 *There are now a number of purpose-built tracks where the sport is very popular. Photo: Roger Nicholson*

2 *Shale track 80–100m in circumference*

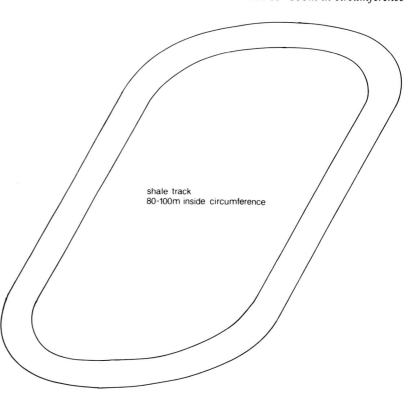

shale track
80-100m inside circumference

57
Fives: Eton fives

1 *The old fives court at Eton, c. 1870. A hand-ball game played by pairs in a three-walled court. Eton fives is played at over 50 centres throughout England, mainly in London, the Midlands, and the south-eastern counties of England, and in Australia, Malaysia, West Africa, and Europe. It is one of three versions of the game, each named after the public school of its origin. (See also Rugby Fives, on p 72). Photo: Country Life*

2 *Space diagram of an Eton fives court. Courts vary in dimensions, but all have a ledge running across the front wall making a horizontal line 1·37m from the ground. Running across the court is a shallow step 3·05m from the front wall, dividing the court into an inner or upper court and an outer or* lower court. *The lower court is 4·65m in depth and 4·27m wide. At the end of the step, projecting from the left-hand wall, is a buttress (known as 'the pepper box'). The upper court slopes downwards approximately 125mm in 3m from the back wall to the step*

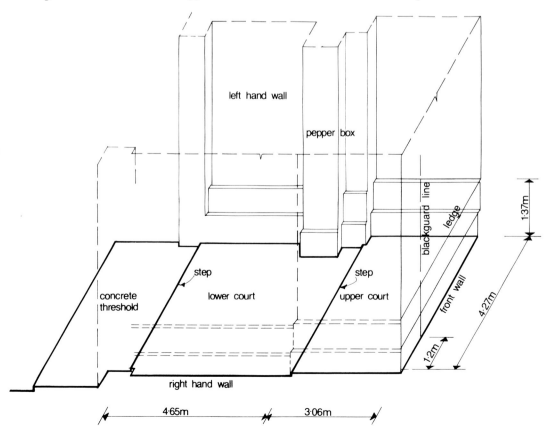

58
American football

1 *Giants versus St Louis. Photo: Colorsport*

2 *American College Football field. Broken line surrounding the rectangular field is the limit line 1·5m outside the playing area. Goal posts are at least 6·1m high; the crossbar is 3·05m above the ground. American Professional football goals are 5·6m wide and situated on the goal line—otherwise the pitch is as for the college game*

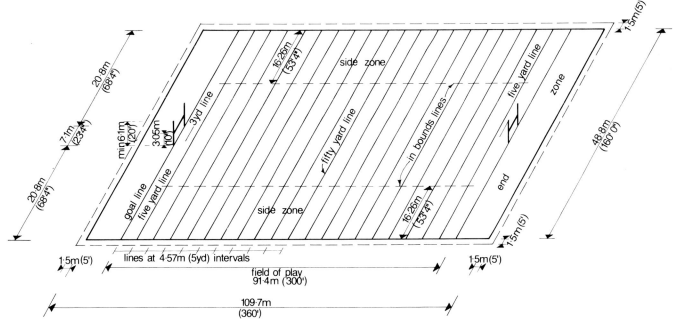

59
Association football

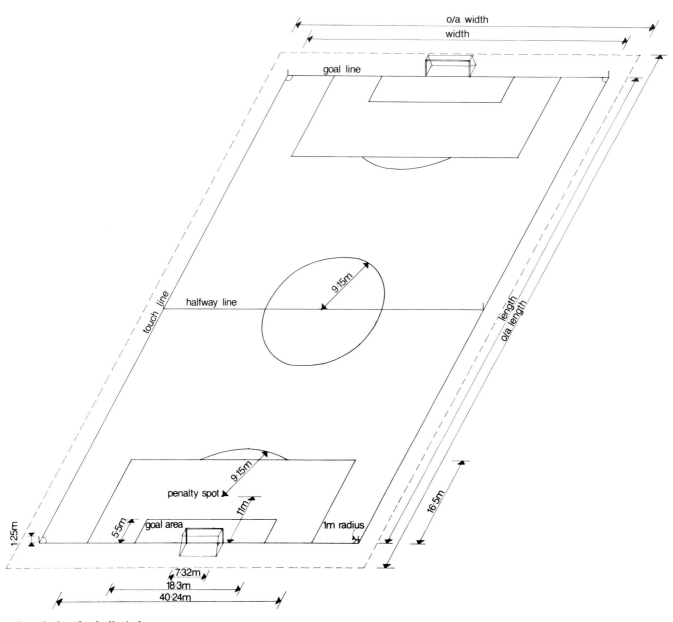

1 *Association football pitch*

3 *Soccer on a local non-turf surface kick-about area. The Football Association considers kick-about areas to be vitally important to football since without casual play areas real skill is unlikely to be developed to the highest possible extent. Photo: Brian Lincoln*

Standard of play	Dimensions (m)					
	Length	Width	End margin	Side margin	Length overall	Width overall
FA International matches	100–110	64–75	—	—	—	—
FA UK matches	90–120	45–90	—	—	—	—
Schoolboy international	75 min.	55 min.	—	—	—	—

NPFA recommendations based on normal practice

Seniors	96–100	60–64	9	6	114–118	72–76
Juniors	90	46–55	9	6	108	58–67
Schools:						
5th year and older pupils	91–96	50–59	6	4·5	103–108	59–68
3rd and 4th year pupils	82	46	6	4·5	94	55
1st and 2nd year pupils	73	41	6	4·5	85	50

English Schools FA

Inter-association trophy competition and under 16 individual schools championship	82	55
Under 19 schools championship	82 min.	64 min.
Primary schools, 9–13 year olds	70–80	40–50

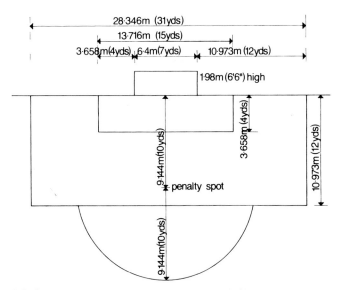

2 *Primary school pitches. Penalty area to be reduced to two-thirds normal size. Penalty spot 9m (10yds) from goal line. Goal 6·5 × 2m (21' × 6'6")*

60
Australian football

1 *Playing field with team formation, Australian rules football. Goal posts (G) and behind posts (B) are 6·4m apart; goal square is 9m deep, square at centre is 45·72m along each side*

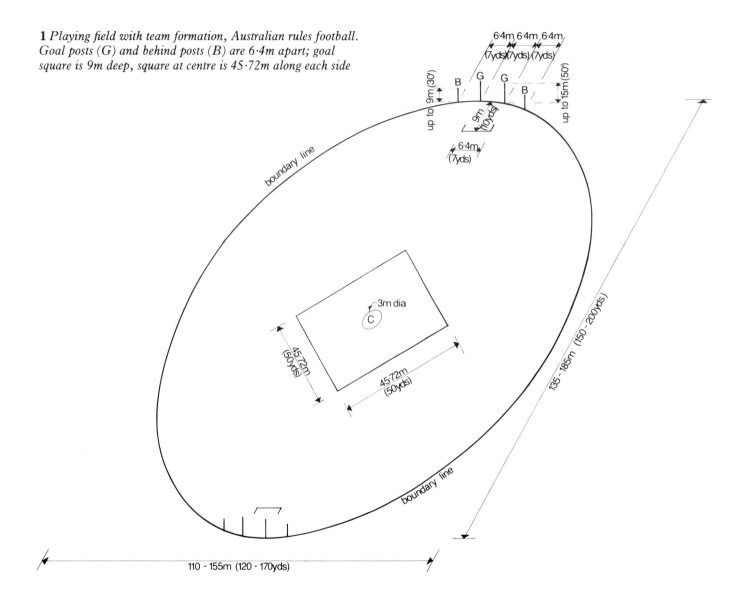

61
Gaelic football

1 *Gaelic football is a 15-a-side ball-and-goal game which, superficially, looks like a compromise between Association Rugby and Football. It is played almost exclusively in Ireland, although British and American teams compete in the All-Ireland championships. Photo: Hugh Brady*

2 *Space diagram of a Gaelic football pitch. Goal area is also known as the parallelogram. Since 1974 an additional outer 19 × 13m parallelogram has been in operation inside which a penalty is awarded for a personal foul only, whereas any foul within the inner goal area concedes a penalty*

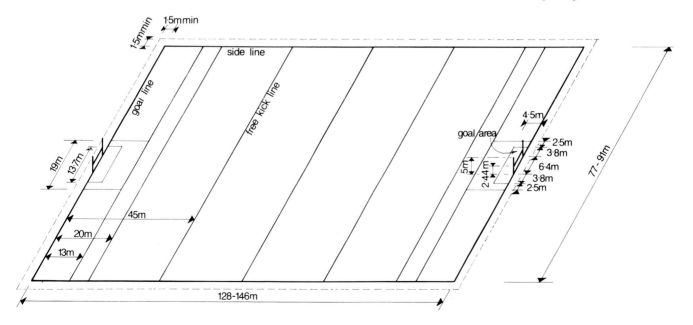

62
Rugby League football

2 *Rugby league football pitch. Note: Side and end margins are 6m. Goal post uprights must exceed 4m. Height from ground to crossbar is 3m*

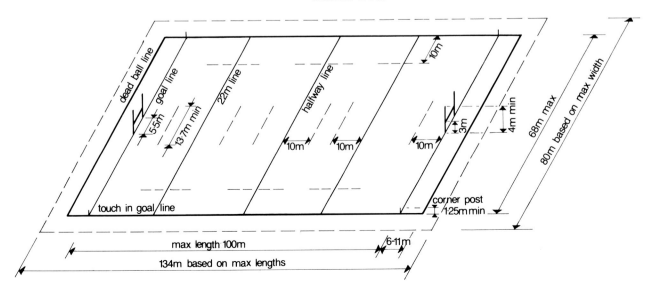

63
Rugby Union football

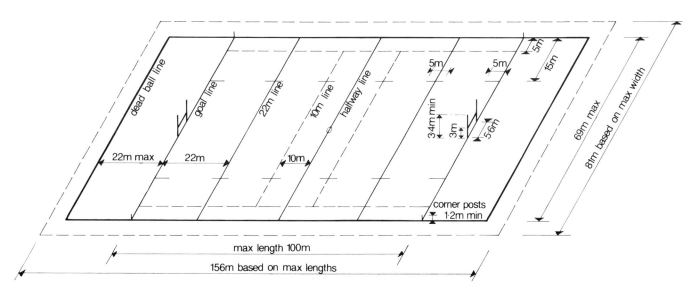

1 *Rugby union football pitch. Note: Side and end margins are 6m. Goal post uprights must exceed 3·4m. Height from ground to crossbar is 3m. Corner posts have a minimum height of 1·2m.*

NPFA recommend pitch sizes for schools

	Length	In goal depth	Width	End margin	Side margin
5th year and older pupils	91–96m	9m	55–59m	3m	4·500m
3rd and 4th year pupils	82m	6·500m	50m	3m	4·500m
1st and 2nd year pupils	73m	6·500m	46m	3m	4·500m

64
Handball

1 *Handball is a no-contact game, played either out of doors (field handball) by two opposing teams of 11-a-side or indoors by teams of 7-a-side or 5-a-side (see Data Sheet 11, p 28). It is played with one or two hands by catching, interpassing, and throwing the ball. Photo: Colorsport*

2 *Space diagram of a field handball pitch. In the 11-a-side version the goal is an exact replica of the Association Football goal. The side of the goal facing the field is painted in alternating light and dark segments, zebra-stripe fashion*

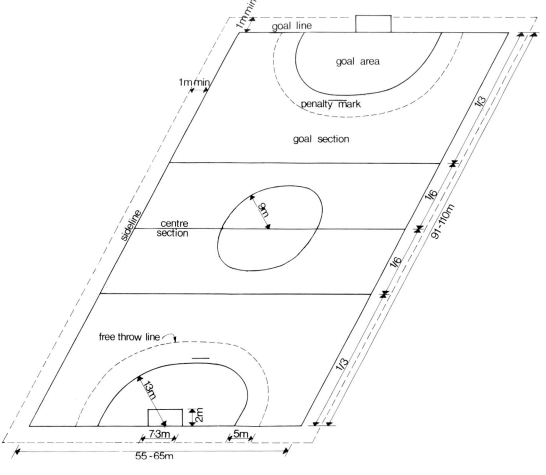

65
Hockey

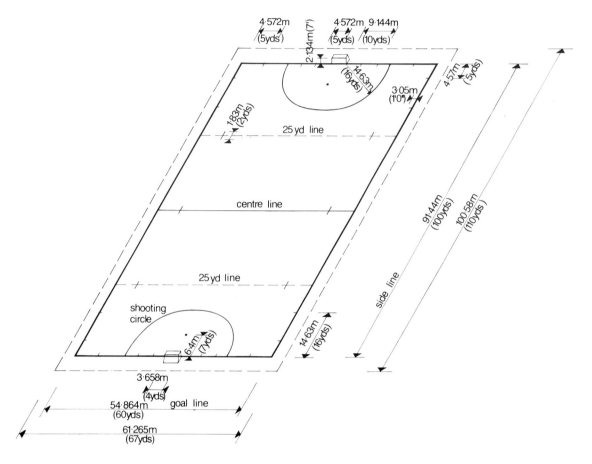

1 *Hockey pitch. Note: height from ground to goal crossbar is 2·1m (7ft). Pitch markings are the same for men and women. Side margin is 3m (10ft), end margin is 4·5m (15ft)*

NPFA recommended pitch sizes for schools

5th year and older pupils	90–100 × 55–60yds
3rd and 4th year pupils	90 × 55yds
1st and 2nd year pupils	80 × 50yds

66
Mini hockey

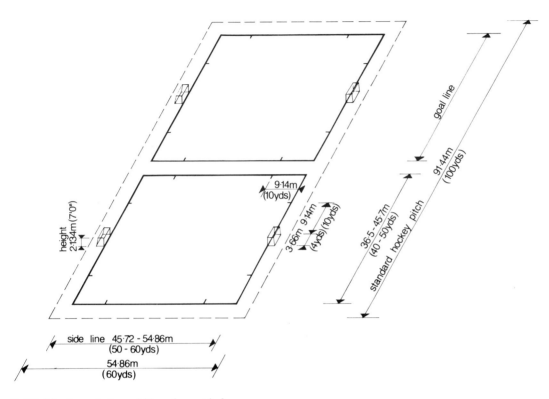

1 *Mini hockey pitches within a large pitch*

67
Hurling

1 *Hurling, certainly the fastest of all team games, is played 15-a-side with sticks and ball. Traditionally a pastime of the Celts, it is still the national game in Ireland, where in places the style of play has many affinities with the Shinty of the nearby Scottish Highlands. Junior coaching. Photo: Seamus McGratton*

2 *Space diagram of a hurling pitch. Dimensions and line markings are very similar to Gaelic football*

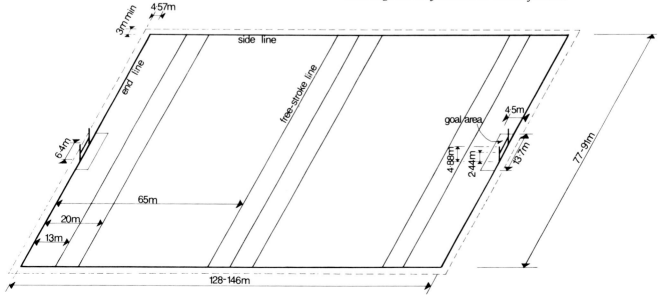

68
Korfball

1 *Korfball is a type of handball of Dutch origin, usually played out of doors between teams of mixed sexes. Six men and six women form a korfball team and at the start of the game these players are divided between the three areas of play, called divisions, i.e., two men and two women in each division. The goals are baskets fixed at the top of posts firmly planted in the ground in each end division. Photo: British Korfball Association*

2 *Space diagram of the pitch. The ideal playing area is a rectangle 90 × 40m level and of short, sharp grass. If necessary smaller sizes are permitted for young players or where the available area does not allow for a full-size pitch. A feature of the game is the marking of the two cross-lines, which divide the pitch into three equal divisions*

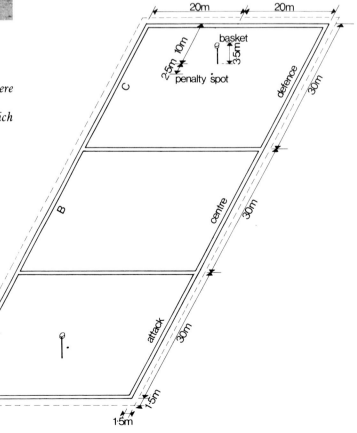

69
Lacrosse: men's

1 *Photo: Roger Price*

2 *Men's Lacrosse pitch. Note: Side and end margins are 3m.*

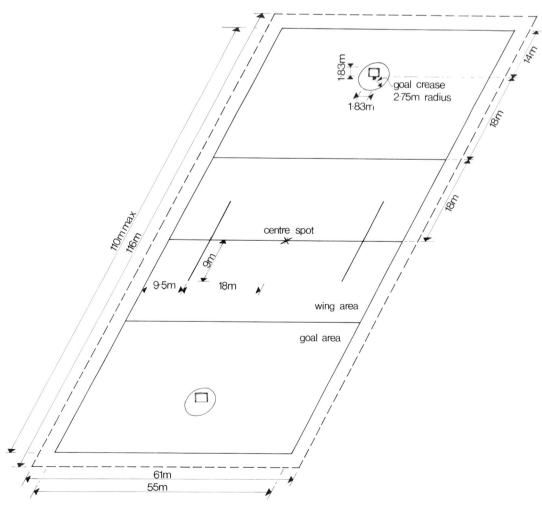

70
Lacrosse: women's

1 *Photo: Phil Sheldon*

2 *Women's lacrosse pitch. Note: the plan shows the minimum desirable area, ie, 110 × 60m. Length between goals is 92m. Length behind goals is 9m. The boundary lines are not to be marked in. For reduced dimensions on restricted pitches and kickabout areas see Lacrosse, p 37*

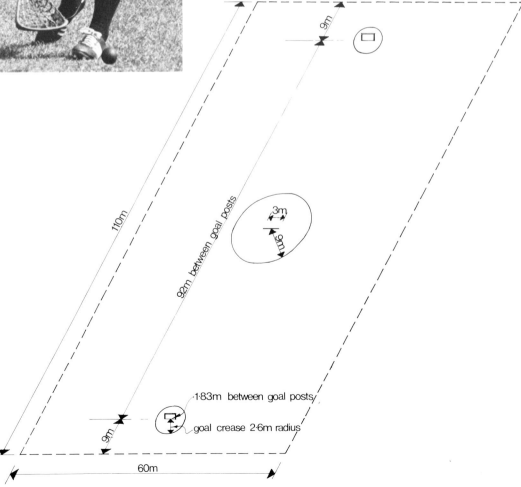

9m

110m

92m between goal posts

3m

9m

9m

1·83m between goal posts

goal crease 2·6m radius

60m

71
Lawn tennis

1 *Lawn tennis court. (Note: facilities for lawn tennis are covered in Volume 3)*

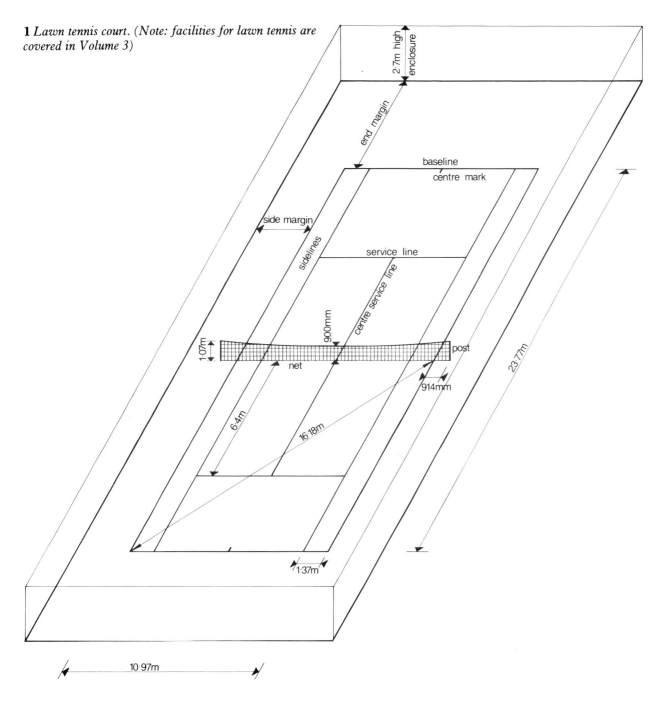

Enclosure dimensions relating to standards of plans (as per LTA requirements)

	International and national official championships	County and Club recommended	Recreational
Minimum end margin	6·400m	6·400m	5·490m
Minimum side margin	3·660m	3·660m	3·050m
Minimum enclosure size for one court	36·580 × 18·290m	36·580 × 18·290m	34·750 × 17·070m
Width for two courts in one enclosure	—	33·530m	31·700m
Width added for each additional court	—	15·240m	14·630m

72
Netball

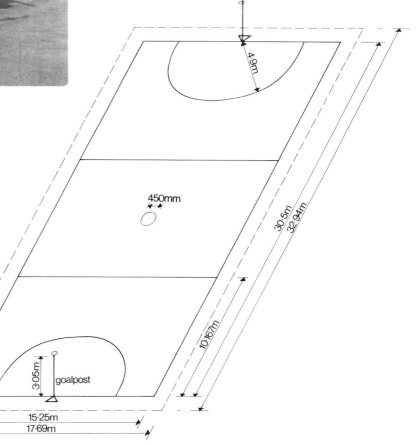

1 *Photo: Brian Worrell*

2 *Netball court. Note: minimum margin at sides and ends is 1·220m*

73
Polo

1 *Photo: Neilson McCarthy*

2 *Polo ground. Dimensions shown are those of a full-size ground including the safety area, which should be at least 4·5m (5yds) beyond the touch lines and 18·3m (20yds) at either end*

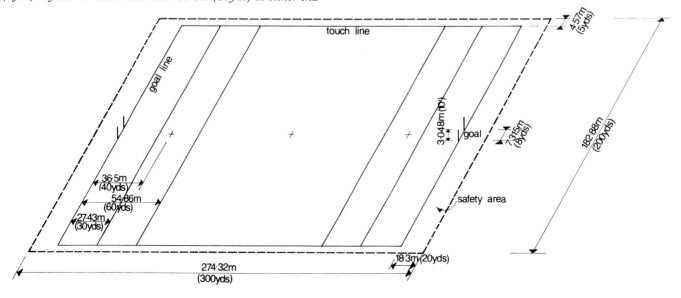

74
Riding and equestrianism

*The British Horse Society (BHS) basic requirements for a riding centre include: a covered riding school (see Data Sheet 40 on p 83); an outdoor manege, **1**; a dressage arena, **2**; a show jumping arena, **3, 5**; cross country fences; riding and hacking paths or tracks giving access to the countryside; stables with saddle or tack room; forage and general stores; manager's office; lavatories and washing facilities; canteen with clubroom; living accommodation; car and horse box park, **4**.*

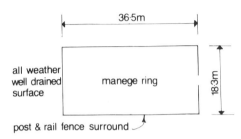

1 *An outdoor manege. An all-weather surface is important, surrounded by post and rail fencing*

2 *Dressage arena. The broken line indicates that spectators and cars should be at least 15–20m away from the arena*

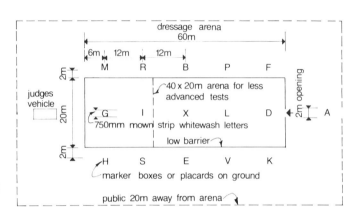

3 *Show jumping ring. If space is tight, the officials and commentary point can share one end with a smaller collecting ring. A warm-up and practice jump ring is also needed, and possibly a clear-round jumping ring, and a separate gymkhana area. Nearby space is required for catering tents, portaloos, trade stands or mobile suppliers, St. Johns Ambulance, vetinary, and the horse box lines. These can total about 1–5 hectares of land*

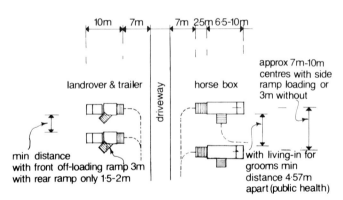

4 *Parking and loading spaces for horse vehicles*

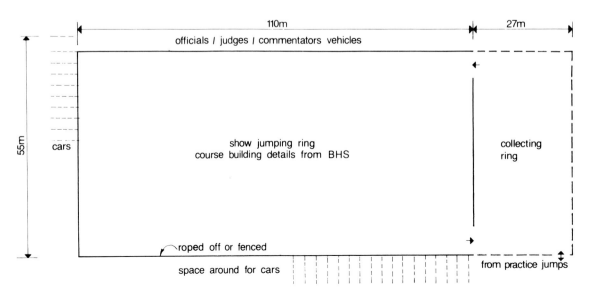

5 *Photo: George Cameron*

75
Roller hockey

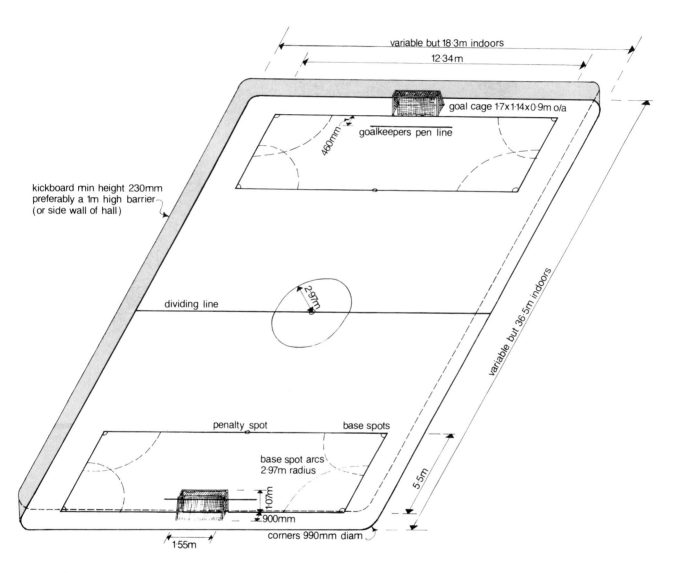

variable but 18·3m indoors

12·34m

goal cage 1·7x1·14x0·9m o/a

goalkeepers pen line

460mm

kickboard min height 230mm
preferably a 1m high barrier
(or side wall of hall)

variable but 36·5m indoors

dividing line

2·97m

penalty spot

base spots

base spot arcs
2·97m radius

5·5m

1·07m

900mm

1·55m

corners 990mm diam

1 *Roller hockey is a team game played on roller skates with sticks and a ball, adapted from field hockey and ice hockey. Sprint speeds of approximately 48km/h are achieved in this fast, keenly contested game, but serious injuries are rare. Owing to the varying sizes of roller skating rinks it is not practicable to lay down a hard and fast rule for the overall dimensions of the playing area, for this is automatically determined, but the size of the penalty area and goal cages are constant. A reasonable playing area would be 36·5m × 18·3m but the ideal is 42·7 × 21m. There is a 230mm high barrier around all sides*

76
Roller skating and speed skating

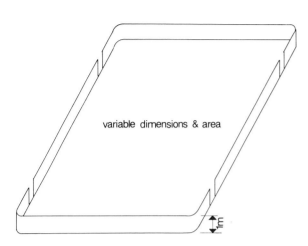

1 *Space diagram of a rink for roller free skating and artistic skating. For roller skating rinks there are a variety of finishes that will give a satisfactory result, each finish having concrete as the material for the structural slab. Essentially the floor must be smooth and level with as few joints as possible and where joints are provided great care must be exercised to avoid lipping. For further details refer to the Cement and Concrete Association's Concrete for Sports and Play Areas*

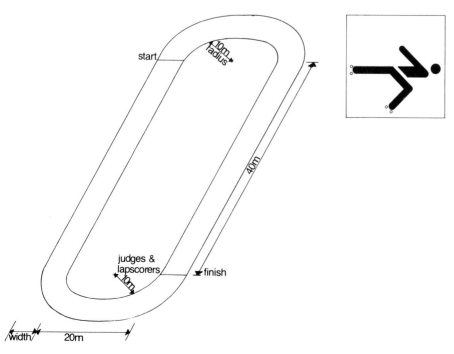

2 *Space diagram of speed roller skating rink. The width of the track limits the number of racing skaters in each heat: 2·44m = 2 skaters, 3·66m = 3 skaters, 4·57m = 4 skaters, 5·49m = 5 skaters, 6·10m = 6 skaters.*

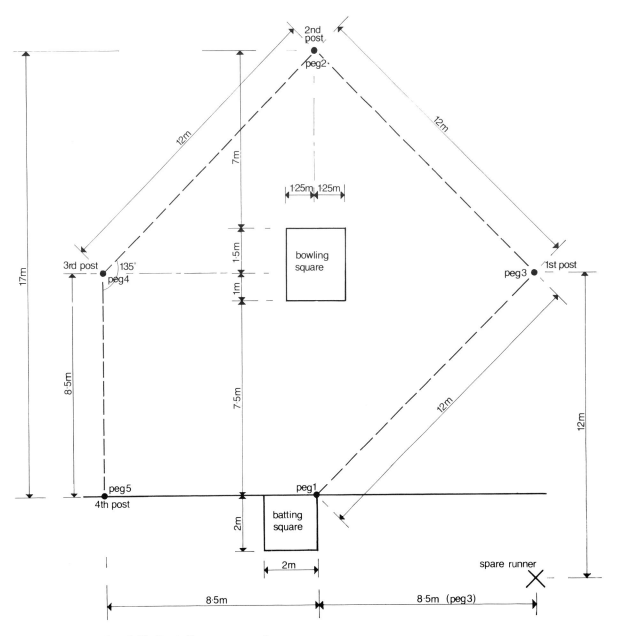

1 *Plan of a rounders field. Dark lines are compulsory markings. Broken lines are peg setting out lines*

78
Shinty

1 *Shinty is the popular name for 'camanachd', the native stick-and-ball game of the Scottish Highlands, originally the same pastime as Irish Hurling. The two games have drifted apart in development and technique through the centuries. Modern shinty is played 12-a-side. Photo: Donald Mackay*

2 *Space diagram of a shinty pitch. The ideal size is 146 × 73m. Further details can be obtained from the Scottish Sports Council*

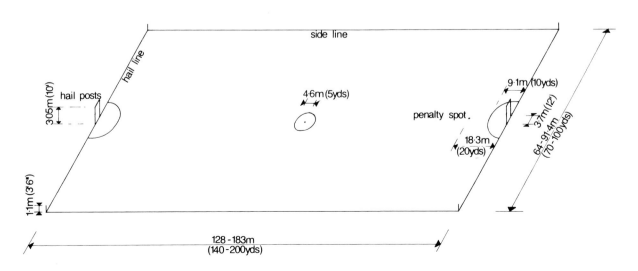

79
Stoolball

Stoolball is an 11-a-side ball game played largely in junior schools in southern England, but also, and increasingly by women, particularly in Sussex and Surrey where the County Association organise a league championship. Scoring and rules are similar to those of cricket, although simpler.

1 Diagram of a stoolball pitch. The striker at the top wicket (i.e. stake, and face board) faces bowling from the bottom bowling crease, and vice versa. The face board is 13mm thick and protrudes 6mm from the stake. The stake is painted black at the bottom to a distance of 0.3m from the ground into which it is driven, on the running crease

300mm
300mm
faceboard thickness 12mm
stake
1.4m
600mm
running crease

9.15m

bowling crease
900mm

14.75m

bowling crease

9.15m

faceboard protrudes
6mm from stake
25mm
stake
running crease

80
Tchouk-ball

1 *Tchouk-ball is an outdoor or indoor non-contact sport. For details and the dimensions of the one-way and two-way versions of the game see Data Sheet 20 on p 42. Photo: Eamonn McCabe*

81
Tug-of-war

1 *Photo: Colorsport*

2 *Diagram of a pull area*

rope off an area approx 46 x 5m (min)

min 32m rope

4m tug

4m tug

2m 2m winning line

List of manufacturers and suppliers

Introduction

S. Wernick & Sons Ltd.,
Russell Gardens, Wickford, Essex, and Lindon Road, Brownhills, W. Midlands
Tel: Wickford 5544 Telex: 5544
Tel: Brownhills 4226 Telex: 339827
Manufacturers of the timber system building to serve your exact needs from small pavilions to multi-storey clubhouses.

Part I Indoor common space activities

Gymnastic Equipment Engineering Co. Ltd., Hampden Works, Milngavie, Glasgow
Tel: 041–956 2233 Telex: 778936
Manufacturers and installation specialists of all indoor sports activity equipment.
Rotunda Limited, Holland Street, Denton, Manchester M34 3GH
Tel: 061–336 4433 Telex: 667763
Manufacturers of self adhesive tapes for sports court markings, electrical insulation, masking, protection and packaging. Rotunda lane marking tapes are particularly recommended for sports court layouts.

5 Bowling: the short mat game
Arnold Wyer Indoor Bowling Greens, Greenhill Industrial Estate, Hurcott Road, Kidderminster, Worcs. DY10 2RN
Tel: 0562 3711
Wygreen '77' for roll-up bowling mats to Irish or other bowling standards. Carpet bowling mats and bowls also available. Advisory service on these games.

7 Cricket
Sports Surfaces International Ltd., P.O. Box 7, Liverpool L24 1UY
Tel: 051–486 5036 Telex: 627080
Uni-Turf for cricket, most major cricket schools in Britain including the MCC indoor school at Lords.

21 Tennis: lawn tennis
Sports Surfaces International Ltd., P.O. Box 7, Liverpool L24 1UY
Tel: 051–486 5036 Telex: 627080
Uni-Turf, the finest tennis surface, gives safety—fast—true sports surfacing for all sports.

22 Trampolining
Nissen International (Sports Equipment) Limited, Tallon Road, Brentwood, Essex CM13 1TT
Tel: Brentwood (0277) 221122 Telex: 995737
Manufacturers of a complete range of gymnastic and trampoline equipment, weight lifting equipment and games equipment for all indoor sports.

Part II Indoor exclusive space activities

37 Rackets
Shaft Sports Ltd., Winrigg House, Borrowcop Lane, Lichfield, Staffs
Tel: 05432 28874 Telex: 337045
Shaft squash rackets, the Shaft 250 for general purpose play and constructed for hire in sport centres. Other rackets include the Shaft 500 and 750 series.
Shaft badminton rackets include the Carbon-Graphite Shaft, the Shaft Shadow and Silver Shaft.

Part III Outdoor activities

EP Publishing Ltd., Bradford Road, East Ardsley, Wakefield, West Yorkshire WF3 2JN
Tel: 0924 823971
Books—'Know the Game' series—over 90 titles; aimed for beginners; illustrated; price 70 pence.
EP Sport series—for advanced players and coaches; over 30 titles; illustrated; £4.95
Full list available from publisher.

46 Athletics
Sports Surfaces International Ltd., P.O. Box 7, Liverpool L24 1UY
Tel: 051–486 5036 Telex: 627080
All levels of athletics, flat or banked tracks, porous or non-porous.

51 Cricket
Ruberoid Contracts Limited, 305 Chiswick High Road, London W4
Tel: 01–995 8093
Ruberoid Cricket Pitch: Tough all-weather, maintenance-free surface for matchplay and practice.
Topcourt: Resilient integrally coloured, porous synthetic surface, providing year round play for tennis and other sports.
Sports Surfaces International Ltd., P.O. Box 7, Liverpool L24 1UY
Tel: 051–486 5036 Telex: 627080
Nottinghamshire pitch and Sherwood pitches for permanent and temporary installations.

65 Hockey
Sports Surfaces International Ltd., P.O. Box 7, Liverpool L24 1UY
Tel: 051–486 5036 Telex: 627080
Primaplay rubber and Nottinghamshire grass porous hockey pitches.

66 Mini-hockey
Ruberoid Contracts Limited, 305 Chiswick High Road, London W4
Tel: 01–995 8093

Ruberoid Cricket Pitch: Tough all-weather, maintenance-free surface for matchplay and practice.
Topcourt: Resilient integrally coloured, porous synthetic surface, providing year round play for tennis and other sports.

70 Lawn tennis: tennis

Ruberoid Contracts Limited, 305 Chiswick High Road, London W4
Tel: 01–995 8093
Ruberoid Cricket Pitch: Tough all-weather, maintenance-free surface for matchplay and practice.
Topcourt: Resilient integrally coloured, porous synthetic surface, providing year round play for tennis and other sports.
Sports Surfaces International Ltd., P.O. Box 7, Liverpool L24 1UY
Tel: 051–486 5036 Telex: 627080
Nottinghamshire grass porous non-turf courts.

71 Netball court

Ruberoid Contracts Limited, 305 Chiswick High Road, London W4
Tel: 01–995 8093
Ruberoid Cricket Pitch: Tough all-weather, maintenance-free surface for matchplay and practice.
Topcourt: Resilient integrally coloured, porous synthetic surface, providing year round play for tennis and other sports.

73 Riding and equestrianism

Sports Surfaces International Ltd., P.O. Box 7, Liverpool L24 1UY
Tel: 051–486 5036 Telex: 627080
Flooring, walling and racing surfaces to absorb energy.

General suppliers

Agility Sports Products Limited, Sportag House, Rotherfield, Crowborough, East Sussex TN6 3HP
Tel: Rotherfield (089 285) 2722
SPORTAG Linkamats for judo, gymnastics, aikido.
SPORTAG Portapost system for netball, badminton, tennis, volleyball.
SPORTAG table tennis tables.
SPORTAG play-fit games. Excel Physical Fitness products. Artificial Grass.
Altrosport Surfaces Ltd., Caxton Hill, Hertford SG13 7NB
Tel: Hertford 54212
Altrosport—a complete range of the most advanced synthetic surfaces for indoor and outdoor use.
Altrosport installed the track at the National Indoor Stadium, Cosford and over 30,000 sq metres of our surfaces were installed for the Moscow and Montreal Olympics.
Grandstand Tribunes Limited, Unit 6, Ffrwdgrech Road, Brecon.
Tel: Brecon 5411 Telex 497730
Suppliers of demountable tiered seating and crowd control barriers for hire or purchase, and fixed stadium/lecture theatre/cinema seating.
Isokinetic Equipment Ltd., 21 Derwent Road, Eastbourne
Tel: 0323 638851
Complete advice, supply and back-up service for isokinetic exercise apparatus.
Isokinetic apparatus: Does not use weights; is very safe to use; can be supplied in portable form—exercise room can be quickly cleared for other use; has proved to be highly efficient in producing improvements in physical power and endurance and in reducing body fat.
Rainham Timber Engineering Co. Ltd., 44 Ferry Lane, Rainham, Essex RM13 9DD
Tel: Rainham (040 27) 55361 Telex: 897512
Suppliers and fabricators of timber engineering products. Technical representation available throughout the United Kingdom.

Bibliography

1. *Sport: A Guide to Governing Bodies*, Sports Council Information Centre 1977. Second updated edition being prepared.
2. Governing bodies of sport handbooks and technical publications.
3. *Rules of the Game*, Diagram Group and Diagram Visual Information Ltd., 1974.
4. *The Oxford Companion to Sports and Games*, John Arlott, Oxford University Press 1975.
5. National Playing Fields Association, revised drawings of outdoor pitches and courts 1980.
6. *IES Lighting Guide: Sports*, Illuminating Engineering Society 1974.
7. 'A programme for the Development of National Sports Facilities': Sports Council unpublished draft May 1979.
8. Directory of Sports Centres and Halls in the United Kingdom, Sports Council Information Centre, 1978.
9. *Facilities for Athletics: track & field*. NPFA/AAA Jan. 1981 (2nd edition).
10. TUS Data Sheets 30–35 'Concentration of Resources—sports', Sports Council, 1981.